Wellness

HIS WAY

Wellness
HIS WAY

Learn to Steward Your Body with God, His Way and for His Glory

Caren Fehr

gatekeeper press™
Columbus, Ohio

WELLNESS HIS WAY:
Learn to Steward Your Body with God,
His Way and for His Glory

Published by Gatekeeper Press
7853 Gunn Hwy, Suite 209
Tampa, FL 33626
www.GatekeeperPress.com

Library of Congress Control Number: 2022940723

ISBN (hardcover):
ISBN (paperback): 9781662929403

eISBN: 9781662929410

CONTENTS

ACKNOWLEDGMENTS

To my husband, Graham:

Thank you for being my biggest cheerleader. When it came time to publish this book, you didn't even flinch at the investment because you saw its value right away. I am so thankful to have you as my companion here on earth. I love you.

To my sister in love, Alysha:

You're the one who saw this as a book when I only saw it as a simple PDF document. Thank you for saying yes to being the very first editor. You took that role so seriously and did it with wholehearted devotion. You saw how this book could be a tool in God's hands to break the bondage so many women are under when it comes to their health. You may be younger than me in age, but that means nothing. I have been so blessed, encouraged and challenged by your wisdom and spiritual maturity! I love you!

To my sweet friend, Nyla:

I am so thankful for your immediate obedience when the Lord prompted you to edit this book for me in its later stage when things got a little slow. Your notes were so encouraging, and I believe made this book even better. Your excitement helped me end the delay and move forward again. I am grateful for you and love you!

To my Wellness His Way Studio sisters:

This book project started as a resource for you. Thank you for allowing me to serve and come alongside you in your walks with God and health journeys since 2015. Even though I may have the title of your "coach," the role I take most seriously is being your sister in Christ. I truly have learned so much from your steadfastness, honesty, perseverance and obedience. You make me better! I love each of you!

To the She Works His Way ministry
(That's you, Michelle Myers and Somer Phoebus!):

Thank you. Your commitment to discipling women in the working world and teaching them to live, serve, work and do all things God's way has had a tremendous impact on my life. I have soaked in so much of what you've taught and applied it to all I do for God's glory, including the stewardship of my body. You have helped shape the way I share and teach the Word of God. Much of what I share in this book has been the result of what the Holy Spirit has done in my life through your teachings and encouragement. Keep running the race faithfully! I love you and the whole team!

BEFORE YOU READ

*H*i, friend! I am so excited about the journey with Jesus you are about to go on alongside this book. I can think of no better way to start our time together than with full transparency and a confession: I have always been the kind of reader that skips the introduction of most books. I find I just want to dive right into the content! Maybe you can relate and are already tempted to skip this part. Or maybe you're getting ready to send me an email on how valuable introductions are, and you would be right. Introductions give the reader a glimpse into the heart of the author and the purpose of the book.

If you are tempted to skip, I am going to encourage you to lean in with me and start slow. Diving right in isn't wrong or bad. But easing in allows us to prepare our hearts and minds more intentionally.

Interestingly, I began this writing project with the Lord in October 2020. Guess what I left last to write? Yup. The introduction. I left it to the very end for two reasons.

First, I wanted to give God room to pivot the purpose of this book as the writing went on. If I had a specific introduction already written, it might have prevented me from staying in step with Him and prioritizing His agenda above my own.

Second, I am very aware that the introduction can either pull you in or push you away. Talk about pressure! It got into my head a little bit. Though I still feel a bit intimidated, I am pressing in and pressing on because I know that God's grace and power are the fuel behind my efforts, and He is sufficient.

There are four things I would like you to know before you read.

1. Why health?
2. Why this book?
3. Why now?
4. Why *His* way?

Why Health?

Because it's a good thing, we may not think that our health can become an idol. But when a good thing becomes the main thing, it's now an idol because we are pursuing and loving it more than God. I love how Tim Keller defines an idol: "An idol is whatever you look at and say, in your heart of hearts, 'If I have that, then I'll feel my life has meaning, then I'll know I have value, then I'll feel significant and secure.'"[1]

With this definition in mind, is anyone else getting slightly uncomfortable? Have you ever found yourself saying, "If I just have this body or lose this much weight, then I'll have meaning, value, significance and security?"

We were never meant to find significance apart from our Creator. Yet, I tried. From 2008 to 2016, I attempted to live God's way *and* my way. It wasn't an "*or*" issue for me but an "*and*" issue. I loved

God so much but struggled to fully submit every part of my life to Him; to walk with Him and His way, and do all things for His glory. Health was one area that I did not want to surrender. You see, I wanted to do it my way and yet also somehow for His glory. I wanted to take all the shortcuts, try all the fad diets, chase weight loss, and *then* glorify God with *my* success.

2012 was the bottom of my valley, my darkest night. I was drowning in a pit of depression and anxiety. My mental and physical health were spiraling out of control. I reached the end of myself and begged God to open my eyes, humble my heart, and pull me out of the pit. I will never forget the amount of weeping I did on my living room floor that day. There was conviction, grace, cleansing and healing. I was ready to confront the sin in my heart, and God was right there to help me overcome it. I got to know, see and experience who Jesus really was in my darkest night.

I know what it is to take care of my body for God, but not with God. I know what it is to compartmentalize the Holy Spirit. It took four years for the Holy Spirit to renew my mind around the topic of wellness (hello, hidden layers). As He did, He began to open the doors for me to share His way with others. The only reason I am here writing a book about doing wellness with God and in His way is because of His redemptive power in my life. He is so abundantly good.

Why This Book?

For many, health is either a stronghold or a stumbling block. It can be too daunting to start or too addicting to surrender. It can be something we could not care less about or something we care too much about. Is there a middle within the extremes? There is, and that way is paved with surrender, discipline and grace. It cannot be discovered apart from God, nor can it be sustained without Him.

As God began teaching me how to live and care for my health with Him, His way, and for His glory, He brought me others to point toward Him. This kickstarted a community I created called *Wellness His Way,* where I could serve and support women who wanted to submit this area of their lives to the Lord.

I would also like to make it clear that this is not a book filled with strategies to lose weight faster or to find the perfect Christian diet approach. Instead, this book is about walking with God and putting an end to the temptation of health becoming something we obsess over or neglect.

The hope is that, whether you read it in its entirety or go straight to the chapters you feel you need most, in this book you will discover God's way in how to view, treat and use your body, as well as how to do *all* things with Him (Philippians 4:13), His way (John 14:6), and for His glory (1 Corinthians 10:31).

Why Now?

Putting it plainly, we live in a world that loudly preaches, "Do *your* thing, *your* way, and for *your* gain." The fitness industry is no exception. If we're honest, deep down we do prefer doing things our way. It's easier and faster. It's more comfortable and convenient. Best of all, it does not require us to die to our selfishness.

The bait of instant gratification, pleasure and recognition appeals to our flesh. We become convinced that is true freedom. So we take the bait because we are blind to the hook. Before we know it, this body God has given us to be another vessel for His glory is now misused for our gain.

Why *His* Way?

Simple: because *He* is God. It's His way because He is *the* Way. It's His way because He is *the Truth*. It's His way because He is *the Life*.

In this book, we will see how differently we live when we do all things *with* God, *His* way, and *for* His glory. "With God" literally means with Him. Walking with Him, trusting Him, seeking Him, and waiting on Him all capture the "with Him" journey. We will also discover together how God's way is not a list of abstract rules or a set of dos and don'ts. It's an expression of His own character and nature. We come to know His Word so that we can wholly seek Him and gain fellowship with Him.

Knowing God is the answer. I am not speaking of just head knowledge, but the kind of *"know"* that includes abiding; a oneness. We cannot fear what we do not know. We cannot love what we do not know. We cannot follow what we do not know. Do you truly know Him? In the first chapter, we will begin here. After all, all creation was created in a way where it can never fully understand itself and know its identity and purpose apart from its Creator.

I also wanted to make sure I took time to clearly state the gospel truth I believe. You will see this referred to often throughout the book, using words such as *believe*, *know* and *follow*:

I believe God created us and desires to have a relationship with us. But our sin separates us from God. Therefore, Jesus took the punishment our sins deserved. By His death and resurrection, Jesus atoned for our sin and secured our justification by grace, not by our works. If we repent from our sins and trust in Christ for our salvation, we will be forgiven, justified and accepted freely by His grace, indwelt with His Spirit until we die and go to heaven.

When I refer to believers, I am referring to those who have understood their sin, have looked to Christ in faith for forgiveness and acceptance, and are daily being regenerated in the new birth by the work of the Holy Spirit! Eternal life is a free gift that, if you haven't received it, I hope this book can point you in the direction of Jesus only!

How to Approach This Book

Now that you have hopefully gained a little insight into the journey we are about to go on, I want to encourage you to grab a journal and document your reflections, what God reveals to you, and the scriptures you want to meditate further on. Even more importantly, I highly suggest you have your own personal Bible open as you read each chapter. I will never claim to understand the gospel perfectly. I am still learning and growing in my personal journey. Therefore, I encourage you to test everything I have written against the Word of God itself. Only the Bible is the *whole* Truth.

With this in mind, each chapter will be broken into four parts:

1. **Strong in Spirit:** Where we will lay down a biblical foundation
2. **Healthy in Body:** Where we will cover practical wellness applications
3. **A Prayer**
4. **Reflection Questions:** Where you can more intentionally examine your heart and take the next best step with God

I love how 3 John 2 (in the Amplified version) says: "Beloved, I pray that in every way you may succeed and prosper and be in good health [physically], just as [I know] your soul prospers [spiritually]." This scripture is the heart behind the two focuses of "Strong in Spirit" and "Healthy in Body."

I will be referring to the New International Version (NIV) of the Bible throughout the book. However, there will be times I share a different translation, in which case I will mention which one. If you don't see a specific translation mentioned, then assume it's NIV!

I cannot wait for God to work in and through your life the same way He continues to do so in mine. Know that while I may not know everything about you, God knows it all and loves you. He is able and willing to redeem and renew the way you view your health as you commit to doing it with Him, His way, and for His glory. I have already been praying for you the same way I pray for myself: that God will be your supreme treasure, that you will come to love His way, that you will no longer attempt to compartmentalize your health or do it apart from God, and that God will be glorified in and through every part of your life, which includes your health.

His Way > My Way

*W*e are daily encouraged to follow our hearts, feelings and understandings. While God did give us emotions and a brain, until those things are submitted under the authority of Christ, they will be faulty sources of wisdom and lead us astray.

I want you to think about the last time you were sold the message of living your way. Maybe it went something like this:

> *"You are in control of your destiny, so you do you!"*
> *"Find your truth."*
> *"Happiness is the highest level of success."*
> *"It's your life, so live it your way."*
> *"Do what's right for you."*
> *"Do whatever makes you happy."*

I'll be the first to put my hand up and admit that I have fallen for these messages. So much of my life, especially my health journey, was filled with the determination to achieve my definition of happiness and success. I even found ways to read God's Word in a way where my will, way and preferences could still lead.

I've discovered that the temptation to live our way grows when there is still a desire (no matter how small) to serve ourselves. But when we set our hearts and minds on knowing God, living His way, and glorifying Him only, He brings *real* meaning and significance to every detail of our lives. While the world will continue to daily offer attractive substitutes, nothing can ever compare to the value of a genuine, intimate and growing relationship with Jesus Christ. May we have the desire to be led and choose to radically follow Jesus and choose His way completely and without reservation.

STRONG IN SPIRIT

Choosing God's way is ultimately choosing life. In order to follow His way, we must know it. To know it, we must know Him. To know Him, we must know His Word. As we come to know Him as He truly is, there is greater joy in denying ourselves so we can wholly follow Him.

Know God

I don't know that there is anything more important than knowing God. God longs for you and me to know His voice, His truth, and His love.

> *Be still, and know that I am God. I will be exalted among the nations. I will be exalted in the earth!*
>
> —Psalm 46:10

We read this verse often and focus most on the aspect of being still, so we miss the reason behind our stillness: *knowledge* of who God is. The direction of our lives is most influenced by what we know and believe about God. It is our greatest privilege in life, and it's what drives our delight in glorifying Him. Knowing Him *is* the foundation of living His way.

I want you to think about how sheep follow their shepherd. Have you ever looked up how sheep come to know their shepherd's voice? If not, this might be the coolest Google search you do today! The point is, sheep don't just follow anyone. Once they come to know their true shepherd, they will not follow anyone else's voice or guidance. Because they know their shepherd, they grow to trust and follow the shepherd's way wherever, whenever, whatever.

Trust is the fruit of our relationship with God and our experiential knowledge of Him and His trustworthiness. Think about this with me. The God who formed you, cares for you, and sent His Son to die for you, desires to have a real relationship with you. He longs to be known by you. Through the amazing sacrifice of Jesus, we can truly know Him like any other person we encounter on a daily basis.

Knowing God is also so much more than simply knowing about Him. For example, I may know all about the mechanics of how rollercoasters work, but I won't know the full experience of a rollercoaster until I actually ride one. In the same way, while it is wonderful to know about God's character and attributes, wouldn't you say there is a difference between knowing about God's love and experiencing His love for yourself?

When we believe and receive each truth regarding who God is, meditate on it, and allow the meditation to lead us to praise and prayer, we can then fully experience and know Him. There is a more intimate sense of "oneness" when we know God and embrace just how loved and known we are by Him.

As we seek to know God, the Bible is clear that we begin to experience all He is. We can hear His voice (John 10:27), experience His love (2 Thessalonians 3:5), and receive His peace (John 16:33). We can experience His freedom (2 Corinthians 3:17), partner in His purposes (1 Corinthians 3:9), and fully rest in His presence (Psalm 91:1).

Know His Word

The best way we can know God's way is by knowing and growing to love His Word. The Bible provides us with various principles for walking successfully with the Lord and in His way.

> *Blessed are those whose ways are blameless, who walk according to the law of the Lord. Blessed are those who keep his statutes and seek him with all their heart—they do no wrong but follow his ways. You have laid down precepts that are to be fully obeyed.*
>
> —Psalm 119:1–4

In May 2020, I made the decision to intensively study the Psalms. When I reached Psalm 119, I noticed how often Scripture was referred to. Out of the one hundred and seventy-six verses, God's Word is mentioned one hundred and seventy-one times and always in connection to God Himself.

I admired how the psalmists yearned, meditated and loved God's Word. I realized that while love cannot be forced, it can be cultivated. God's Word is worth cultivating love for, simply because God's Word is God's heart.

How do we cultivate such love? By making it our highest priority. Once something becomes a priority, we make time for it and give it our attention and care. We cultivate love for God's Word by reading it, meditating on it, bending our minds to it, honoring it, obeying it, and thanking God every day for it! I have seen firsthand how being in God's Word daily positively influences every other decision I make.

I always loved my dad's encouragement to me when I was cultivating my own love for God's Word. He encouraged me to ask three questions while reading scripture:

1. What does it teach me about who God is?
2. What does it teach me about who I am?
3. What does it teach me about my enemy (Satan)?

These three questions help me make sure that when I am reading God's Word, I never forget that its primary purpose is to reveal God's character and way to me. We never want to be so focused on how the Bible applies to our circumstances that we miss how it displays the character and heart of God. The more that God Himself is our greatest desire, the less we will misinterpret or twist Scripture to meet our needs.

Denial of Self

Whoever wants to be my disciple must deny themselves and take up their cross and **follow me.** *For whoever wants to save their life will lose it, but whoever loses their life for me will find it.*

—Matthew 16:24–25

The path of self-denial is paved with humility and ultimately addresses who is on the throne of our hearts. I love how Greg Ogden describes self-denial in his book *Discipleship Essentials* as not a denial of our brain or feelings but a denial of self-lordship.[1] God will not share the throne of our hearts with any other lowercase god. Not even a little.

When He is on the throne, we do everything for His glory. When we are on the throne, we do everything for our gain. To put it plainly, when we follow Jesus, we turn from our way, which represents our old life, and follow Jesus and His way, which represents our new life in Christ. Faith is the only way we can do this. It is by faith that we come to believe that God is who He says He is and will do what He promised. This leads us to surrender our will entirely, including our thoughts about how our lives should be. As we surrender, our lives become about so much more than a checklist of our accomplishments and instead are a reflection of His life, love and grace. True fulfillment comes when we decide to love God more than anything else and give Him all of ourselves.

Unfortunately, we've warped Jesus's command to deny ourselves a more comfortable and less sacrificial experience. Rather than radical obedience, we've chosen conditional obedience. We read "deny yourself" and in our minds twist it to "deny some of yourself."

This was me. I denied some parts of me, while other parts I kept my way. It was easier to make Jesus an add-on—a part of my life—rather than the point of it. Or, as my friend Michelle Myers once said, "Jesus was never meant to be an addition to our lives but the foundation of our lives."[2] Yes and amen.

When we search His Word, we discover that our heart was created wholly by Him and wholly for Him (Colossians 1:16). We cannot find true meaning apart from Him. Therefore, fighting to gain the world without Jesus will lead to a life of restlessness, anxious striving and emptiness (hello, Ecclesiastes). Yet, when we deny our old life entirely and come to a deeper knowledge of who He is, we will joyfully deny anything that hinders us from choosing Him as our supreme treasure.

Follow Him

As we come to know God, know His Word, and deny ourselves, we begin to see how following Jesus cannot be a casual thing we choose when it's convenient or comfortable for us. Jesus is no longer just one important thing in our lives; He is most important. Following Jesus means we turn from our way to follow His way *completely*.

Sometimes we can fool ourselves into thinking that we can follow Jesus with zero surrender, zero cost, zero self-denial, zero pain and zero repentance. Friend, this is not following Jesus. This is us following ourselves and trying to convince Jesus to follow us.

Following Jesus with wholehearted devotion means we no longer attempt to live our way *and* His way. It means we've counted the cost of following Him because He doesn't hide the cost from us. It means we accept the cost with joy because He also doesn't hide the eternal reward from us.

Jesus is the only way! He is the way to the Father, the way of life, and the way to salvation. Jesus lived on earth to show us the way.

He gave us His Spirit to continue reminding and teaching us of His way. I love how Greg Ogden reminds us that the Holy Spirit is radically Christ-centered, and His ultimate mission is to make us radically Christ-centered too.[3] May we grow to love Him and count everything else (including weight loss) as loss compared to knowing Him.

HEALTHY IN BODY

Let's pause here for a moment. Are you by any chance already thinking, "Wait a minute! I thought this was a book about exercise and eating!" I'm thinking you skipped the intro where I explained a few important housekeeping matters? Caught you! I encourage you to go back to look over the intro (it's not long, but it's very important!). But if not, here is the CliffsNotes version: we need to lay some groundwork rooted in Christ before we can start talking about approaching wellness with Him.

I am tempted to say trust the process, but I'm sure this is a phrase you've heard a million times and may leave you wanting to chuck this book across the room. So I'll say this: Lean into the whole journey. We need to address the heart, mind and spirit first in order to get to the body with a healthy mindset. Give each one fair care. Can we agree on that together?

In addition, there's a purposeful reason why in each chapter we always begin with Strong in Spirit before we get to Healthy in Body. God's Word and Truth should saturate our very being and change how we do everything, including taking care of our body!

Now that we've cleared that up and covered what God's way means and looks like in our Strong in Spirit section, we can now approach the topic of wellness together with greater wisdom. *Total* commitment to Christ influences how we redeem our time, abilities, relationships, and, yes, our health.

When we know God, know His Word, deny our flesh, and follow Him, we become Spirit-led, not self-led. This changes what we do and how we do it. I can't help but think of Paul's words in Philippians 3:8: *"What is more, I consider everything a loss because of the surpassing worth of knowing Christ Jesus my Lord, for whose sake I have lost all things. I consider them garbage, that I may gain Christ."*

This is a picture of someone who is so devoted to knowing God that everything else is less than. What would it mean to consider weight loss or specific body image compared to the surpassing worth of knowing Christ? What does it mean to consider them garbage so we may gain Christ?

It doesn't mean we neglect our bodies; it means we do all things with a spirit of excellence to gain more of Christ, be more like Christ, and for the glory of Christ.

Compartmentalized Devotion

I think we can all agree that the fitness world is a dark place. If not surrendered to the Lord, the journey of wellness can quickly go from *Christ*-centered to *self*-centered. As I shared in the introduction, for many years I thought I could compartmentalize the Holy Spirit and choose what areas He could transform, heal, and make me more like Jesus. Can you guess what area I refused to surrender? Health. The two main reasons were pride and fear.

My lack of knowing God on an intimate and reverent level left me convinced that I knew my body better than the maker of it (oof). I didn't think God wanted to be in those tiny details. Besides, fitness was a good thing. It couldn't possibly become an idol, right? Wrong. Through a long self-inflicted valley, I learned that the moment we decide to control something and remove God as the foundation of it, we step into idolatry territory. In Exodus 20:3, God says, "*You must not have any other god but me.*" If we aren't seeking *first* His Kingdom, we will start building our own kingdoms. We were made to be followers, but not followers of our dreams, desires or the next fad diet. We were made to be followers of *Jesus*.

Fear was the second reason I struggled to surrender my health to the Lord. I didn't want to face the possibility that I had made fitness my idol. Satan loves to magnify our mess, minimize God's grace, and use accusation to leave us in a pit chained by guilt and shame. In contrast, God lovingly convicts our hearts so we have an opportunity to humbly repent so He can restore. Again, a deeper knowledge of God's character and what His Word says enables us to disarm those lies and fears.

I tried doing it the world's way for God's glory, and doing it my way *and* His way. Neither worked in the long term. In fact, those other ways only took me on a path of deeper bondage. We simply cannot run two races. We either choose His way or our way, but we cannot choose both. We will either be loyal to honoring the Lord with our bodies or loyal to honoring our flesh and preferences.

His Way vs. the World's Way

Here are some examples of how God's way is starkly different from the world's way and why you cannot choose both:

The world says, "Depend on yourself."
God says, "Depend on Me."

The world says, "Do whatever you please."
God says, "Do what pleases Me."

The world says, "Worship your body."
God says, "Worship Me with your body."

The world says, "Your body is an accessory."
God says, "Your body is My temple."

The world says, "External beauty is everything."
God says, "Beauty is fleeting."

The world says, "Strive."
God says, "Surrender."

The world says, "Take the easy way."
God says, "Enter through the narrow way."

The world says, "Save your life."
God says, "Lose your life."

The Bible is countercultural and unpopular. No matter how hard you try to marry the world with His Word, it won't work because His Word is set apart and holy. As you can see from the list of above examples, you cannot run both races. You must choose one.

Health His Way

Christ must rule over every part of our lives. Following Him totally means we surrender all we do totally. Health is no exception. If health is not an area where Christ is your center, my hope is that this book leads you to a place where He is, and that wellness becomes another vehicle to magnify Him.

Your wellness journey can build godly character *if* that's your focus! God can use it to make you more like Him as you yield to His way for you in it. You can show up to train your body today, while remaining available to the Holy Spirit who trains your character in godliness.

Just remain cautious. While God can use physical training, so can the enemy. It comes down to motives and where your eyes, heart and focus are. Physical training can easily lead us down a path of pride, toxic comparison, distraction, discontentment and bondage. The natural drift is for it to become self-centered (our way) more than Christ-centered (His way). Frequent heart and motive checks are necessary!

With this in mind, while workouts and proper nutrition can change your physical body, only Jesus can transform your heart and renew your mind. It starts by taking any other lowercase gods (idols) off the throne of your heart, joyfully surrendering your life to Jesus, and making Him the point of your life.

Before moving on to the next chapters, I'm purposefully using this first foundational chapter to invite you to deeper self-examination. Are you only wanting to add God to your journey of wellness, or do you want Him to become the foundation you build your whole life upon? It can't be wellness His way *and* your way. You cannot follow Him and yourself. It's His way or your way. Just know that if you choose His way, He will enable you to walk in it.

PRAYER

Father, You are the way, the truth, and the life! Forgive me for the times I choose my way over Yours. Forgive me for only making You an addition to my life rather than the foundation of it. I want to know You so I can better love You and follow Your ways. Help me to follow Your ways and Your plans as You have laid them before me. Give me wisdom to heed Your Word for Your glory, my good, and the good of others. As I begin taking care of this body You gave me, may I rely on You to show me how. Teach me Your way, O Lord. I love You! Amen.

REFLECT

❶ How has your wellness journey been more your way than His way?

....
....
....
....
....
....
....

❷ What thoughts or beliefs keep you from surrendering your whole life (which includes your health) to Him?

....
....
....
....
....
....
....
....
....
....
....

❸ Ask the Holy Spirit to reveal where an area of your life is not ruled by Christ, and pray for the humility and strength to surrender it to Him today.

....
....
....
....
....
....
....
....
....
....
....
....
....
....

CREATOR > CREATION

efore we get to the practicality of *Wellness His Way*, we need to evaluate and ensure that our foundation is Christ, our hope is Christ, our reason is Christ, and our motive is Christ!

It's so easy to fall into the trap of worshiping our bodies rather than using our bodies to worship their Creator. Have you ever thought about how your workout could become an extension of your worship? Let's put an end to striving to do good works apart from the abiding presence of our Creator and examine what parts of our lives need to have a greater connection to the love of our God.

STRONG IN SPIRIT

Your Body is a Temple

Do you not know that your bodies are temples of the Holy Spirit, who is in you, whom you have received from God? You are not your own; you were bought at a price. Therefore honor God with your bodies.

—1 Corinthians 6:19–20

These verses are often used when discussing health and wellness. It's not enough to use them to motivate us, only so we can get lost in the pursuit of looking a certain way, achieving a certain size, or making it all about us. If so, we've actually missed the entire point of these verses!

There are four things we can learn from these verses. I'm going to share them in a way where we can see how each fundamental truth leads to the next:

1. We were *bought.* God created us (Genesis 1:27), and then He bought us (Galatians 3:13) when Jesus paid the price for our sin on the cross.
2. We are *not* our own.
3. We belong to God, and He places the Holy Spirit inside those who believe in Him and makes them a temple for His dwelling.
4. *Therefore*, we are to honor and glorify God with our bodies.

When Paul wrote these specific verses in his letter, they were an argument to flee from sexual immorality. His words also reveal the importance of caring for our bodies in a way that never compromises God's glory and all-satisfying goodness.

Michelle Myers puts it this way: "*'My body is a temple'* is about our Creator, not the creation."[1]

The conviction that comes from the awareness that our body is a temple of the Holy Spirit should compel us to ask, "Is the way I am using and caring for my body glorifying God as the Creator or me as the creation?"

Your body is His temple, and it's another vehicle to display His glory and your contentment in Him! One of my favorite quotes by John Piper is, "God is most glorified in us when we are most satisfied in Him."[2] Wow, right? The Creator is most magnified when His creation is most satisfied in Him. We get to display this satisfaction in how we care for our bodies.

I think of Moses's prayer in Psalm 90:14: "Satisfy us in the morning with your unfailing love, so we may sing for joy to the end of our lives."

Moses understood that to experience unfailing joy, he needed nothing else except to be satisfied with God's unfailing love. Unfailing joy isn't going to come from having the perfect body, but from a real relationship with our perfect God.

What if, before we jump into our normal prayers, we begin by asking God to satisfy us with His love and His very Self? How differently would we, as His creations, glorify Him when we are living from a place of complete satisfaction in Him?

His Temple for His Glory

We will be better able to steward our temple for God's glory when we meditate on how Jesus's sacrifice on the cross (which defeated the power of sin and death) allowed God to fill the earth with His presence. Jesus made a way for us to be the new temples of His holy and powerful presence!

The fact that we are now the temples of the Holy Spirit means that we have God Himself in us to love us, heal us, redeem us and lead us. We have access to a more real and intimate relationship with our heavenly Father and Creator. I encourage you to pause right now and take time to rest in the beautiful, real and loving presence of your Creator. As you meditate on the presence of God that dwells within you and makes you a righteous new creation, ask the Holy Spirit to reveal where you may be delighting more in the creation than the Creator Himself.

God Delights in His Creation

I would also like to add that there is absolutely a place for enjoying the creation God has made because God Himself enjoys His creation, especially us! When He created the world, we see Him commenting each time, "It was good," and with man, He said, "It was very good" (Genesis 1).

God delights in us as His creation. He is not anti-pleasure. It's when the pleasure takes His place that we have a problem. Enjoy nature. Enjoy the food He has made. Enjoy the people He's placed in your life. As you do those things, never lose sight of the Creator Himself. We don't worship His creation; we worship Him. Ultimately, the purpose of the creation is to make the most of the Creator because *He* delights in His creation.

HEALTHY IN BODY

Through and for Christ

Now that we've established that we are God's creation and that our highest purpose is to glorify Him, let's zoom into the actual act of caring for His temple.

The Son is the image of the invisible God, the firstborn over all creation. For in Him all things were created: things in heaven and on earth, visible and invisible, whether thrones or dominions or rulers or authorities; all things were created through Him and for Him.

—Colossians 1:15–16

Declare it with me: My body was created through Christ and for Christ! When we believe this, humility protects us from stealing God's glory in our wellness journey, and enhances our awareness that our bodies were created to worship and not to be worshiped. This truth also keeps us dependent on God when making decisions for our health. After all, it would be really hard to take care of our bodies without *daily* (sometimes hourly) consulting the Creator of our bodies.

While I am so thankful for all the resources out there today that help us take care of our bodies, it's become clear that not all approaches work for everyone. We have been given unique bodies, which means a resource that works for others may not work for you. I have also seen how quick we are to first seek Google's thoughts on the best diet before we seek the counsel of our Creator.

I used to be the girl who would spend two to three hours just jumping from one article to the next on how to lose weight, stop binging, and have the perfect nutrition plan. Not once did I pause to ask God to show me His way for my body. Why? This feels so ridiculous to admit, but truthfully, I felt like God's answer would be something super-spiritual when what I felt I needed was something practical. I thought, "I just need ten tips, the perfect plan, a list of foods to eat and foods to avoid, and a strong will. That's it!" Anyone else just so incredibly grateful for God's patience? And mercy? And grace? And all the things He is? Yeah, me too.

My journey took a major shift in my heart, mind, spirit and body when I learned to ask God to show me *His way* for my body. I learned to go to my Father *first*. My Creator. My Redeemer. My Savior. My Friend. My Shepherd.

You Have What You Need

Your hands made me and formed me; give me understanding to learn your commands.

—Psalm 119:73

Friend, your body was formed by God's hands, and He knows what you need to take care of it well. Our culture today is constantly switching gears to the latest fad. Here's the thing, though: God's design for your body and its nourishment was established before time began. He is able to guide you toward a better understanding of the basic wellness principles He created.

What would it look like if you started asking the Lord for wisdom when considering how to take care of your body, mind and spirit His way? His way is not one of striving but surrender. His way is more concerned with our obedience than the outcome. His way is paved with love and truth-filled conviction that aims to restore by His grace. His way is not of shame, guilt or condemnation. Simply put: His way is nothing like the world's way.

You have what you need to see positive change in your health journey because you have Jesus. You have the Creator in you, with you, and for you. If you're stuck in a parking lot of despair, frustration, and repetition of habits that you know hinder your life, Jesus comes near and whispers: "You can move from this place, but you must be leaning into Me."

Seek Him and you will find Him when you seek Him with *all* your heart (Jeremiah 29:13). Not sure how to handle your relationship with sweets? Ask Him how He would have you engage with sweets. Not sure how to start moving your body? Ask Him for wisdom on the best type of movement for your body in this season.

God invites us to draw near to Him and seek Him in the big and small. So why not start today? What questions do you have? Bring them to Him.

Make Jesus Known in Your Wellness

My prayer today is that you experience the beauty, wonder and peace that comes from worshiping your Creator with your very body. I pray that today will be the end of the perpetual thirst you've been experiencing because you've been looking for satisfaction everywhere else but in Jesus. My prayer today is that your wellness will become an extension of your worship and witness to make Jesus known as the Creator and Sustainer of all things!

Before you tell me there's no way to make Jesus known through something like our workouts or stewardship of our bodies, here are three examples:

Habakkuk 1:7(?) [handwritten margin note]

1. We make Jesus known and glorify Him in our wellness journey when we remain content and satisfied in Him, even if the scale never moves *(Challenge: Insert your own personal "even if___")*.

2. We make Jesus known and glorify Him in our wellness journey when we use our bodies to serve others, and make decisions for our bodies that enhance, not hinder, our capacity to serve.

3. We make Jesus known and glorify Him in our wellness journey when our wellness decisions become less about how we want to look and more about who we want to praise and honor.

Let's seek Him, honor Him, and be fully satisfied in Him today.

PRAYER

Father, You are the creator of all things, and You sustain all things. All things were created through You and for You, and this includes my body! Thank You for Your gift of salvation and for giving me Your Holy Spirit to dwell in me. Make me more like You and teach me the way to go. Forgive me for loving the things You've made more than loving You. Forgive me for focusing so much on the gifts that I've neglected to glorify You as the Giver. All I am and all I have is Yours. May you be glorified through this body and through the way I live today. I love You! Amen.

REFLECT

1 Is the way you are using and caring for your body glorifying God as the Creator or you as the creation?

....
....
....
....
....
....
....
....
....
....

2 How does the statement "My body was made by Christ and for Christ" change the way you care for it?

....
..........Mindshift..
....
....
....
....
....
....
....
....
....
....

❸ What is one way you can practice making Jesus known through your wellness journey?

....
....
....
....
....
....
....
....
....
....
....
....
....
....

STEWARDSHIP >
OWNERSHIP

We often connect the topic of stewardship to finances and our work, but have we ever considered the stewardship of our bodies? Confession: Stewardship was never my goal or motive when I started taking care of my health in 2009. It was all about what I could achieve, the weight I wanted to lose, the confidence I wanted to gain, the way I wanted to look, and the approval from others I wanted to receive. In short, it was all about me.

Selfish ambition fueled my pursuit of wellness and led to a long and dark valley. I experienced depression, anxiety, insecurity and despair. In 2015, I reached the end of my rope (where God does His best work) and *finally* surrendered. I released all the pressure I had been carrying, trying to do God's job. There is a reason He is the owner and we are the managers. We as the creation cannot sustain what we did not ordain. What we can do, however, is steward what God ordained and rely on His enablement to manage it with Him, His way, and for His glory.

STRONG IN SPIRIT

Not Our Own

In his book *Mere Christianity*, C.S. Lewis writes, *"Every faculty you have, your power of thinking or of moving your limbs from moment to moment, is given to you by God. If you devoted every moment of your whole life exclusively to His service, you could not give Him anything that was not in a sense His own already."* [1]

Everything you and I have has been given to us by God. *Everything*. Our spouses, kids, money, bodies and possessions all belong to God. Humor me for a moment and just hold up your hand and look at it. Who owns your hands? God does, because He made them! Doesn't this change how you want to use your hands?

> *You are not your own; you were bought at a price. Therefore honor God with your bodies.*
>
> —1 Corinthians 6:19–20

You and I are not our own. In fact, we are doubly owned. God made us, and then He bought us because of His love. It was God's love that drove Him to create the world, and it was His love that drove Him to save the world. He sent His only son Jesus, who knew no sin, to be sin, to take our punishment on the cross so that whoever believes in Him will not perish but have everlasting life. Jesus lived the sinless life we can never live and died the death we deserve.

In another letter addressed to the Galatians, Paul says, *"I have been crucified with Christ and I no longer live, but Christ lives in me. The life I now live in the body, I live by faith in the Son of God, who lived me and gave himself for me."* (Galatians 2:20) Paul understood that his life wasn't his anymore. It now belonged to Jesus Christ! He no longer owned his life. Instead, he got to manage the new life Christ gave Him with the Holy Spirit.

Friend, the only way to steward what we've been given from a place of reverence, worship and joy is to reflect on the Giver Himself. That is, who God is, what He has done, and His gift of salvation to all who believe in Him, repent of their sin, and receive His invitation to follow Him.

When we fully believe and receive the truth of the gospel, it changes everything in our individual lives. It changes *why* we live, *how* we live, and for *whom* we live.

The Parable of the Talents

One of my favorite parables that expands on the topic of stewardship is found in Matthew 25:14–30 and is known as the parable of the talents. I would love for you to spend some time reading it slowly and allowing Jesus's words and warning to sink deep into your heart. For the sake of space, I will summarize it here!

In this parable, Jesus teaches that the Kingdom of Heaven is like a master (representing Jesus) going on a journey. Before he goes, he gives three servants different amounts of money (talents) to invest while he's gone. To one, he gives five talents. To the second, he gives two talents. Lastly, to the third servant, he gives one talent. Each is given according to *his* ability. When the master returns and asks how they stewarded his money, the first and second servants reveal that they invested the talents they were given and doubled the master's money. They receive the master's praise. The third servant, who was given one talent, safeguarded the master's money but did nothing to increase it. As a result, he is condemned by the master for his wickedness and laziness.

There is a lot to unpack in this parable, but I would like to highlight a few things that radically transformed my personal "why" behind stewardship.

Out of sheer grace, the master (who wasn't obligated to give his servants anything) *entrusted* what he owned to his servants to manage and steward until his return. Everything was still owned by the master. The servants were merely administrators who would answer for how they invested the master's belongings.

In the same way, God is the owner of everything. All things were created by Him and for Him. By His grace, He gives us certain abilities, gifts and capabilities (talents) to manage and steward for His glory and the good of others until His return. God trusted us *first* by giving us these things.

If you have ever thought to yourself, "Why should I even bother trying when everything God gives me belongs to Him?" or "Since God owns everything anyway, what's the point?" I want you to lean in with me. It's a valid thought! Jesus, in all His wisdom, reveals the answer in this same parable.

The first two servants are examples of faithful stewardship. Because they truly *knew* their master, they felt the importance of the responsibility they were given. Out of reverence for him, they immediately got to work and stewarded his money with intention and faithfulness. The multiplication of what they were given was the fruit of their faithfulness, and they were *ready* for their master's return.

The first two servants understood their position in relationship to their master, and that is what fueled their immediate faithfulness. We, as God's creation, exist for His glory. To exist is to have meaning. For example, what is the meaning of a light bulb that's not in a socket? It may look nice, but ultimately it's meaningless. It's not until the bulb is in the socket that it then lives out its true meaning.

You and I were created to exist and carry the image of God. It's His glory that gives us value and *real* existence. We never existed before God decided that we should exist. We would never have existed in eternity if Jesus didn't pay the price for us to exist there as well. When we truly grasp this truth, we begin to joyfully submit to the true meaning of our lives, and that is to serve, glorify and magnify our Master. He's the socket that, when plugged into, we find our true meaning and identity.

Since the first two servants understood that their purpose was to work in the best interest of their master, they were able to come into the joy of their master, and their power and authority grew. The one in control of two was promoted to be in control of four. The one in control of five was promoted to be in control of eleven.

The third servant, though, unfortunately did not grasp his life's true meaning. He did not truly know the master. Therefore, he played it safe and hid what he was given, working for his best interest rather than the master's. His lack of faithfulness (and laziness) prevented fruitfulness and did not honor his master. We can learn two additional lessons from his actions:

1. Sometimes we allow our misunderstood views of God to justify or excuse poor stewardship and disobedience. The third servant had an inaccurate view of the master because he did not truly *know* him. There was no reverence for him. As we saw with the master's reply, that excuse didn't pass. I assume it did not pass because the master never hid who he was or left his character up for interpretation. His character was clear; otherwise the first two servants would have misunderstood him too.

2. We must remember the truth of God's character while reading Scripture. Because we know God is just and good, this means that the master's harsh rebuke was justified. It wasn't rash or undeserving. He knew the third servant's heart. God meets our weakness with His grace (2 Corinthians 12:9), but this wasn't a weakness issue for the third servant. Remember God gives each according to his ability. With this in mind, we can conclude that it wasn't that the third servant wasn't able, it's that he wasn't willing.

3. In verse 25, we get the sense that the third servant was proud of his decision to do nothing when he says, "See, here is what belongs to you." Sometimes we do "complacency" with excellence and deceive ourselves into thinking it's true excellence. In other words, we give ourselves an A+ for doing the bare minimum. Since we are bearers of the

image of God, complacency cannot glorify God because God is not complacent. We glorify God when we represent His character and magnify all that He is.

As we can see, a stewardship mindset is impossible until we truly believe that our lives have no meaning apart from God Himself. It's when we humbly accept the reality of being creations for the Creator that we can manage all resources God provides for His glory, rather than for our selfish gain.

HEALTHY IN BODY

Your Body Is a Talent

We can be quick to relate "talent" to more obvious responsibilities like our spouses, kids, work or money. Have you ever thought about your body as being a talent? It is one! You are the only one who can steward your body. That responsibility cannot be delegated, the same way you cannot delegate being a spouse or a parent.

While our bodies are temporary, that doesn't negate that they are still necessary for effective service on earth. While they're not the main thing, they help us do the main thing—love God, love people, and spread the gospel. Our bodies have the ability to enhance or hinder how we love our neighbors, spouses and kids, and serve others well. When we proactively care for them, our bodies allow us to love God and others with the highest capacity.

Neglecting our bodies would be like the servant who did nothing with his talent. In the same way the master asked his servants to give an account for how they used his money, God will ask us to give an account for how we stewarded and invested what He has entrusted to us. Now that we view our bodies as talents, how are we using them to do what matters most (love God and our neighbor)?

"But My Body Is a Problem"

I would like to pause a moment and talk to my friends who feel they've been given a "problem" body. Maybe you're battling against a disease, or it seems like your body is often against you and refuses to lose weight.

Your body is not your enemy or a problem—it's a gift. It will be impossible to steward your body for God's glory if you are unable to view it as a gift from God. Yes, even something that is a challenge can be seen as His grace. It is impossible to faithfully care for what we don't first surrender. It is impossible to faithfully care for what we don't value. A talent was worth a lot in Jesus's time (one talent was worth around sixteen years of labor!). The point being made is that you are never to undervalue what is given to you by God. That includes your body. Do you undervalue your body?

It's also important to note that we cannot steward well what we don't understand. Have you taken time to try to understand your body? What makes it sluggish? What makes it fatigued? What leaves it bloated? When we have the correct view of seeing our bodies as gifts and not as enemies, we can partner with our bodies with kindness, grace and a teachable spirit.

If we are honest, we can be quick to blame God for why we can't take care of our bodies. We deem the bodies we have too difficult to manage. I would love to both encourage you and caution you. As we read, the third servant had the audacity to blame his master's character for his lack of diligence. Not only so, but both his fear of failing and laziness kept him from even trying. The master would have been more pleased had the servant attempted to put the one talent into the bank so it would gain some interest (Matthew 25:27).

If your body has been more difficult to steward, the answer is not to neglect it, be lazy with it, or blame God. Remember, God will not ask you to give an account of the outcome but your *faithfulness*. In the same parable of the talents, we see how each servant was given responsibilities to manage according to his individual ability. God, in His divine wisdom, knows our limits, and by His grace works within and even beyond them. We also see how the master didn't specifically ask the first servant if he doubled the five talents, nor did he compare and ask the second servant if he made as much as the first servant. Each servant was rewarded according to his own faithfulness and labor.

God will not ask you to give an account for things outside of your control (outcome). The question will be, "What *did* you do with what I gave you? How were you faithful in glorifying Me? Did you rely on Me for wisdom, strength and power to take a step toward stewardship?"

A final word of encouragement if you have been discouraged with the body you have. Sometimes God keeps certain illnesses or weaknesses to keep us humble and fully dependent on Him. I think of Paul when he begged God to remove the thorn in his flesh (2 Corinthians 12:7–10). While no one knows what this "thorn" was, we can relate to Paul's struggle.

God's answer was unexpected and perfect: "*My grace is sufficient for you, for my power is made perfect in weakness.*" The very thorn Paul thought would hinder him from Kingdom work, God used to enhance his Kingdom work while deepening Paul's knowledge of God Himself. May this be a sweet reminder to you today that God is able to work in and through our weakness to display His strength.

God-reliant Stewardship vs. Self-reliant Stewardship

God's grace is indeed sufficient. We cannot forget that the renewing of our minds and transformation of our hearts is impossible without Him. I say this because sometimes temptation rises as we steward what we are given: the temptation to strive. We start out meditating on God's Word and enjoying the journey with Him, but somewhere along the way, we let our guard down and start to meditate on the goals we want to achieve and how fast we want to achieve them.

If we leave the motives and power behind our stewardship unchecked, we can go from God-reliant stewardship to self-reliant stewardship. Something that has helped me ensure over the years that I don't get caught in striving mode is having a "symptoms of striving" checklist. I'll share with you some of mine, then I encourage you to write one for yourself!

There are three primary symptoms I experience when I revert to self-reliant stewardship. The first is chasing numbers. I start to allow the scale to dictate every action I make and my food intake. I also start to be overly concerned with how many calories I burn. When my mind is only focused on numbers and it becomes all about what I can burn and what the number on the scale says, I know I am trying to care for my health with my strength and on my terms.

The second symptom is when I refuse to rest. When my body is prompting me to rest and stretch, but I am so focused on the outcome that I push through (the kind of push that doesn't honor the body I have), I know I am striving. Lastly, I get caught up in over-research on how to take care of my body. There's a place for knowledge, but if we aren't cautious, knowledge can feed a striving mindset. I'm sure you have seen how big and loud the "self-help" world is. Everywhere you turn, you're likely to see or read something that tries to convince you that you are the solution to your problems, the source of your strength, and the hero of your story. Suddenly, the concept of healthy self-care and stewardship gets hijacked and twisted into self-reliance and even self-worship.

While we do have a responsibility to be good stewards of our bodies, we must remember that we can't change our own hearts or sinful natures apart from the Holy Spirit's sanctifying work in us! It's only Jesus who offers us the way to real redemption and healing.

Health-based self-help books can offer some helpful insight into how our brains work, the purpose of food, and some ideas for practical application that can help enhance our stewardship, but these resources cannot renew our minds or transform our hearts. I simply want to caution you when you read or listen to things that exist to teach you about your health, weight loss, and your body. When you read these resources, ask yourself:

- Does this align with what God says in His Word?
- Does this move me to depend more on Christ or myself?
- Will the application of what I'm reading or listening to honor the Lord and glorify Him or honor me and glorify me?

Those are my three. Maybe for you a symptom is comparison. Maybe you try to steward your body but use your strength to achieve this person or that person's results. Whatever it may be, lean in and allow the Holy Spirit to meet you there and bring you back to stewardship with Him.

Pursue Faithfulness

Finally, stewarding your body doesn't mean pursuing skinny. Instead, it means honoring God with what you have and pursuing faithfulness. Just because your outcome may look different from the person next to you, it doesn't mean your faithfulness is less.

Even when the outside is slow to change, the inside is transforming when we are led by the Spirit. More than anything else, we must care more about the journey (no matter how difficult) of magnifying Christ and making us more like Christ.

When others see your steadfast faithfulness in caring for your body, *even if* outward results aren't obvious, they will wonder, *why*? Why still care? Why still try? This is where your answer can be: "Because I love the Lord. He gave me this body. Therefore, it's not a burden but a blessing. I get to partner with my body in an effort to prevent it from being a barrier to my ministry here. I get to offer it daily as a living sacrifice unto my Lord and God. He continues to give me the wisdom and strength I need to care for it each day. I know He sees my willingness, and I am becoming more like Him through patience, self-control, peace, gentleness and faithfulness...that is enough."

Take heart, friend! God did not give you things to steward apart from Him but *with* Him. You have access to His wisdom, so ask for it! Rely on the Spirit, not just your own understanding of what your body needs. Focus on your wellness journey being less about achieving goals and more about taking care of the body He created. Surrender everything He gives you back to Him, declaring, "*You* are my Creator. Show me *Your* way to take care of what *You've* given me."

PRAYER

Father, thank You so much for the gifts You have given me—my life, my family, my friends, my body, my time, my talents, and my material possessions. All that I have comes from You. Help me to remember this and rejoice in Your goodness. May I steward what You've entrusted to me in a way that glorifies You, makes You known, and increases my delight in You. This body is Your creation. May each day that I exercise it, nourish it, hydrate it and rest it be with a mindset of stewardship, not one of pride, achievement or ownership. I love You! Amen.

REFLECT

❶ We are called to be stewards of our bodies. Sometimes we pursue God-reliant stewardship, and sometimes we drift into self-reliant stewardship (striving). What do you think is the difference between the two?

....
....
....
....
....
....
....
....
....
....
....
....

❷ Draw a vertical line down the center of a piece of paper and label one side "My responsibility" and the other side "God's responsibility." On one side, identify what your responsibility is when it comes to stewarding your body. On the other side, identify the things that only God can make happen. Are there any things on the God side that you've been trying to achieve yourself? Is there something under the "me" side in which you need to be more disciplined? Take a moment to identify those things you have responsibility over and offer them up to God. Ask Him for strength to be disciplined and diligent in those areas, and to surrender the areas where only God is in control.

....
....
....
....
....
....
....
....
....
....
....
....
....
....
....
....
....
....

❸ With the awareness that your body is a talent, how does that change how you want to steward it?

....
....
....
....
....
....
....
....
....
....

OBEDIENCE > OUTCOME

*O*ne of the most freeing lessons I have learned in my walk with God is the distinction between my responsibility and His. My responsibility is to show up with a willing heart, walk with God, give Him my absolute best, and release the outcome to Him. Do you feel a weight lifted as you read those words? I know I did just typing them!

As I've shared, for so many years my main focus was weight loss, looking good, or fitting into a certain size. Being so goal-focused and success-driven left me in a state of striving. I was exhausted, depleted, and felt constantly defeated. I somehow convinced myself that God wanted me to succeed when His Word never calls us to succeed but to *obey*.

STRONG IN SPIRIT

God Gives the Growth

I would like to invite you to read the parable of the growing seed in Mark 4:26–29. In summary, Jesus tells of a man who scatters seed on the ground and then lets nature take its course. As the man who sowed the seed goes about his business day after day, he finds the sprouts come, then the stalks, then the leaves, then the heads of grain, etc. Jesus emphasizes how all this happens without the man's help. It seems like the man is shocked at how it all happens without his intervention. Verse 28 says, "All by itself the soil produces."

This parable ends with a harvest that grows through the farmer's obedience to plant and water, not through the intervention to bring the growth himself. This teaches us that God can do anything and is always working out the outcome, whether we are aware of what He is doing or not. In His timing and His way, He brings the growth so He alone can receive the glory.

Our responsibility is to humbly plant and water. It's not impressive. It gets messy. It can feel mundane. Yet, wherever God has planted you, you are called to plant.

Abraham's Example

One of my favorite examples in the Old Testament of a life of "Obedience > Outcome" is Abraham. God said to Abraham in Genesis 12:1–3, *"Go from your country, your people, and your father's household to the land I will show you. I will make you into a great nation, and I will bless you; I will make your name great, and you will be a blessing. I will bless those who bless you, and whoever curses you I will curse; and all peoples on earth will be blessed through you."*

If this were me, I would have some questions right away. The promises sound great, but where are we going? For how long? Who should I take along? How will I take care of them?

Abraham may have thought those things, but He chose to trust God, focus on obedience, and let God take care of the *where, why* and *how* (aka the outcome). He focused on what God said instead of what He didn't say. It was Abraham's love for God and his faith that fueled and led to his radical obedience.

The Way to Obey

Genuine love for Christ should always manifest itself in obedience. We don't obey out of obligation and with dread. We obey out of love and with delight. Obedience only feels like duty when it's birthed from a place of religion for God rather than a relationship with God. When we love Jesus with all our hearts and He becomes our everything, obedience is a joy.

I often say to my son, "Obey all the way, right away, and with a happy heart."[1] This is a phrase I learned from Ginger Hubbard's parenting book *I Can't Believe You Just Said That*, and it has stuck with me because it's just as relevant for us as adults as it is for our kids.

We are to:

- Obey all the way—partial obedience is still disobedience.
- Right away—delayed obedience is still disobedience.
- With a happy heart—because of my love for God, my obedience is joyful.

I'd also like to add a quick caution to obedience in general. Obedience sounds good until its motives are not. If our obedience is motivated by what God can do for us rather than by our love for

Him, we've missed it. It's not just that we obey but *why* and *how* we obey. We obey because we love God (1 John 2:3–6). We obey by faith (Romans 1:5).

Some questions to consider:

1. Do we obey because of who God is or because of what we want?
2. Is our obedience flowing out of our faith in the Lord or driven by our works?
3. Do we obey completely, immediately and with delight, or do we obey partially, slowly and with a spirit of duty?

Friend, may we remain faithful and obedient to hear God's "*Well done, good and **faithful** servant*" (Matthew 25:23, emphasis added). Notice it does not say "good and *successful* servant." Ultimately, it is when we are faithful that we are successful, because God's definition of success is obedience.

While obedience often requires courage, we can be confident that God is always there, empowering us to do His will and ready to give us His best as we obey. The reality is, we fall short quite a bit. Praise God for His grace in those situations! Nevertheless, for those who follow Christ, we must commit to obeying God, because it is essential to our faith and is the evidence of our faith. Faith and obedience are inseparable. Let us demonstrate our trust in God by yielding to His will, His way and His glory, today and always.

HEALTHY IN BODY

Specific to your wellness journey, it is so easy to only focus on the outcome. You may be wondering how long it will take to lose the weight, what sacrifices you'll need to make, how hard it will be, or what guaranteed results you'll see. It's tempting to want the results without the surrender or obedience.

What if, like Abraham, you chose to obey no matter the outcome?

There's a reason the outcome is not irrelevant but is "less than." It's not wrong to have the outcome in mind. However, it should be where you glance, not gaze. Keep Christ as the focus of your gaze because your gaze influences your chase. When He is your gaze, you'll seek Him first, find contentment in Him, and stay in step with the Spirit. When the outcome is your gaze, you open the door for striving, control and discontentment.

Worrying vs. Caring

Have you ever considered the subtle difference between worrying and caring about the outcome? In Matthew 6:25–34, Jesus commands us not to worry about tomorrow. Notice He doesn't say "don't *care* about it" but "don't *worry* about it."

I've discovered that the more I care about something, the more I'm driven to my knees before the Lord, and the more I'm willing to take faith-filled action *with* God. The more I care, the greater my posture of surrender is.

But worry? Worry sucks joy and peace from our lives. If we aren't careful, it can dismiss God's presence entirely. Worry can paralyze us from all action or catapult us into hasty and unwise decisions *without* God. Worry can lead to greater striving, while caring can lead to greater surrender.

Testing the Motive of Our Obedience

When I was in "weight loss mode," the Lord brought this question to me: "If the scale never moved, would you remain faithful and obedient in stewarding the body I gave you?"

That question wrecked me. After some time (I'm not even going to pretend I answered this quickly!), I came to the conclusion that, yes, even if my preferred outcome didn't happen, I would choose the purpose of stewarding my health. I would choose obedience because I love the Lord, and I know caring for the body He gave me honors Him, glorifies Him, and enhances my ability to serve others well. I would choose obedience because ultimately I trust God.

This kind of obedience not only helps me persevere and continue to make the next best choice for my health, but also protects me from being seduced by quick fixes and a diet culture mindset. When all we are striving for is the outcome of weight loss or being a certain size, we are more vulnerable to the lies of the fitness industry, such as:

Lie: Stay away from bad food and only eat good food.
Truth: Food has no moral worth. Food is food. It's meant to fuel you, not rule you.

Lie: Without food rules, you'll gain weight.
Truth: Rules may work for a short period of time before they become overwhelming, unrealistic and unsustainable. Flexible boundaries can be beneficial. Rules can be enslaving.

Lie: A certain body image will fulfill you.
Truth: Only Jesus can fulfill you. Everything else will fail you.

Like David in Psalm 139:23, I invite us to come before the Lord, asking Him to search us and know our hearts, to test us and know our anxious thoughts. Testing the real motive behind our obedience will reveal the true condition of our hearts. The more our measure of faith and trust in the Lord increases, the more radical our obedience will be.

Trust and Obedience

With that said, do you trust God in the area of health? Do you trust that His way is higher and better? Do you trust that He is able and willing to help you make time for body care each day (sometimes in different ways), even in a busy season of life? Do you believe He loves you and that He is an ever-present help in times of struggle or trouble? If we don't really know God and believe Him, we cannot trust Him. If we do not trust Him, we will not obey Him.

Psalm 106 taught me this valuable lesson. In verses 24–25, we see the Israelites struggling to believe God's promises, which leads them to grumble in their tents and disobey God. I had never seen the link between belief and obedience before then.

Now when I struggle to obey God in the area of my health, I pause and pray, "Lord, show me where I am struggling to believe You." At times, I struggled to believe that He really cared about how I took care of my body. Then I remembered 1 Corinthians 10:31: *"So whether you eat or drink or whatever you do, do it all for the glory of God."* Other times, I struggled to believe that I could stay consistent with it. Then I remembered Philippians 4:13: *"I can do all this through him who gives me strength."* When I struggle to believe I'll ever see victory in this area of my life, He brings me back to Romans 8:37: *"No, in all these things we are more than conquerors through him who loved us;"* and 1 Corinthians 10:13b: *"And God is faithful; he will not let you be tempted beyond what you can bear. But when you are tempted, he will also provide a way out so that you can endure it."*

Knowing God's Word fuels our belief in Him, and that enables us to trust and obey. So, what would it look like to deliberately trust, submit to, and obey God with your health? The more your trust in Him grows, the more you can take care of your body from a posture of "I get to" rather than "I have to." As you show up to steward well what He has given you, you will start to see how:

- Your wellness journey is another area of your life where you get to depend on God.
- Your wellness journey is another area where you get to practice trusting God with all of your heart.
- Your wellness journey is another area where you get to practice contentment in Christ in all circumstances.
- Your wellness journey is another area where you get to focus more on His glory than your gain.

- Your wellness journey is another area where you get to partner with the Holy Spirit and ask Him to make you more like Jesus through it.

I challenge you today to not just invite Jesus in but also make Him the point of your wellness journey. Walk with Him and work with Him. If you are feeling discouraged because results have yet to come in your health, I encourage you to detach yourself from the results. Anytime the outcome becomes more important than obedience, you've gotten lost in the pursuit of your flesh. Instead, focus on the reason behind your obedience to care for your body (also known as your "why") and do all things with excellence unto God.

For my friends out there who have been struggling to commit to obedience and showing up, I have a few tips for you that have helped me personally:

- Ask the Lord to help you appreciate caring for your body simply because it honors Him!
- Surround yourself with others learning to do it His way. Accountability is key.
- Choose wellness approaches that are simple, sane and sustainable.
- Surrender your health. Commit to it. Then surrender it again.

We don't need to grit and muscle our way through obedience. When we are fully reliant on God's power and grace, we can show up with joy and peace for His glory. Friend, the results will come in time and in the way God created your body to have them. Until then, embrace focusing on faithfulness over fruitfulness. There is a sweet freedom that comes when your health journey is more about Him and less about you! Right now, you can practice the joy of surrendered obedience that comes from your growing trust in the Lord.

PRAYER

Father, You are the God of the harvest and the outcome. You are God and I am not. Help me surrender the outcome of my health journey to your hands. Not only that, but I surrender to you my family, my desires, my resources, my work, and my plans. Forgive me when I desire what You give more than You as the Giver. Forgive me when I treasure the things of this world and forget that You are to be my supreme treasure. May my love for You drive my obedience today, and my trust in You enable me to surrender the outcome with peace. I love You! Amen.

REFLECT

❶ Do you obey because of who God is or because of what you want?

....
....
....
....
....
....

❷ Do you find that you obey completely, immediately and with delight? Or partially, slowly, and with a spirit of duty?

....
....
....
....
....
....
....
....
....
....
....
....
....

❸ How have you noticed unbelief impacting your obedience?

....
....
....
....
....
....
....
....
....
....
....
....
....
....

WITH GOD > FOR GOD

$\mathcal{D}$uring one of my conversations with God while writing this book, it became clear to me how easy and subtle it can be to lose God's way. In both my health journey and in my work as a *Wellness His Way* coach, I've discovered that there are three primary ways we can get lost. The first is doing things *our* way for *our* gain. The second is doing things *God's* way but for *our* gain. The third is doing things *our* way but for *God's* glory.

Confused yet? I promise these will make sense in a moment.

STRONG IN SPIRIT

First, I want to clear something up! It's absolutely true that we are to do all things for the glory of God (1 Corinthians 10:31). But the *doing* for God (action) is the *outcome* of our *walking* with God (having a personal relationship with Him and faith in Him). This is why when focus more on the "with Him", it can lead to an more fruitful "for Him."

Abide

I am the true vine, and my Father is the gardener. He cuts off every branch in me that bears no fruit, while every branch that does bear fruit he prunes so that it will be even more fruitful. You are already clean because of the word I have spoken to you. Remain in me, as I also remain in you. No branch can bear fruit by itself; it must remain in the vine. Neither can you bear fruit unless you remain in me. I am the vine; you are the branches. If you remain in me and I in you, you will bear much fruit; apart from me you can do nothing.

—John 15:1–5

In John 15, Jesus reveals that we can do nothing of eternal value apart from Him, and that we are to remain (also known as abide) in Him. So what is abiding?

- **Connection:** Abiding in Jesus means being connected to Him. This is the union we have. The same way a branch is connected to the vine, and a vine to the branch, we are connected to Christ and He to us. No connection means no life and no fruit.
- **Reliance:** We as the branches get to be dependent on the Vine. There is no such thing as independence in abiding. The branches get their life and power *from* the Vine. Without the Vine, the branches have no purpose or life— they are useless and powerless. We are completely reliant upon Jesus for everything that counts as spiritual fruit. Apart from Him, we can truly do nothing (v. 5).
- **Continuance:** Abiding means to remain, stay or continue. We are to remain in Jesus. We never stop believing Him, trusting Him or relying on Him. Abiding is not a one-and-done event but a steadfastness in our gaze upon Him, our walk with Him, and our attachment to Him.

Therefore, we cannot just bear fruit for the glory of God. We bear fruit because we are first attached to Jesus as the True Vine. When we are humbly walking *with* God, following *His* way, abiding in *His* Word, and relying on *His* power, our faith grows and we magnify Him. It's our love for God and faith in Him that produces faith-filled action (works).

Three Ways We Can Get Lost

Our Way for Our Gain

This one is the most obvious. It describes someone who still has *self* (aka pride) on the throne of their heart. It's all about what we want, how we want it, and how we'll benefit.

If you open up to Luke 15:11–32, you will find the parable of the prodigal son. I encourage you to pause, read it, then meet me back here, because I will be referring to both brothers in these next two sections.

The younger son prematurely asks for his father's inheritance so he can leave and live life on his terms, his way and for his gain. In Jewish and Arab cultures, to ask a father for one's inheritance early is to wish one's father was dead. The younger son ultimately wanted the father's things but not the father himself. He wanted independence, prestige and freedom. It was all about him.

God's Way for Our Gain

Funny story: Initially while writing this chapter, this one wasn't included. It's so subtle I nearly missed it! We see an example of this from the older brother in the same parable of the prodigal son.

While the younger brother was reckless, the older brother seemed faithful. He did all the things his father wanted. He followed his rules and walked in his way. All seems well until the end of the story, when we discover the motive behind his obedience. He didn't obey his father and walk in his way because he loved him, but because his father was a means to an end. He followed his way, but ultimately for his gain and what he could get out of it. The older brother was as equally lost as his younger "our way for our gain" brother. Perhaps he was even more lost because he couldn't see how lost he really was.

Our Way for God's Glory

This one hits close to home and was how I did things for so long: my way for His glory. I wanted to glorify God, but I relied on my confidence, strengths, skills, understanding and emotions to do it. When people asked me why I was taking care of my health, I would say, "For His glory." When people would ask me *how* I did it, I would point them to my way, which really only stole from God's glory. Every part of our lives (even *how we live them)* should point people back to Jesus.

Now that we've established the three ways we can get lost, let's talk about what it actually looks like to walk with God.

His Way for His Glory

It starts by ensuring your relationship with Jesus is the most important one in your life. When it is, it will be harder to wander from walking intimately with Him and being in full reliance on Him. When He is the foundation of your life, you will want to seek Him first, exalt Him, and please Him with all your ways. When He is the only One you follow, you will be more alert to stay in step with Him.

Walk by the Spirit, and you will not gratify the desires of the flesh. If we live by the Spirit, let us also keep in step with the Spirit.

—Galatians 5:16,24

Notice that the more we walk by and keep in step with the Spirit, the better we are able to starve the desires of the flesh. Sometimes we put greater emphasis on not gratifying the flesh and we forget the power that comes from walking closely with God as the basis for starving the flesh. When our greatest desire is to honor the Lord, we become more willing to cut out anything that hinders us from walking in His way.

The more we desire God above all things, the less appealing sin is, because *He* becomes the most satisfying thing. When we want God most, we can deny our selfish desires. When we love God most, we can push off anything that hinders us from living His way.

Walking with God is a daily decision and a way of life. We get to depend on the power and work of the Holy Spirit to enable us to walk with Him! He needs our willingness, but it's His power that makes us able.

HEALTHY IN BODY

One of the greatest dangers we face every day in our lives on earth is the temptation to want things more than Jesus. A heart check is required anytime we find ourselves more focused on appearance and approval in our wellness journey than on glorifying God and worshiping Him with the bodies He gave us.

I invite you to reflect on these three questions to get to the true condition of your heart:

1. Are you committing to your health your way for your gain?
2. Are you committing to your health your way for His glory?
3. Are you committing to your health His way for your gain?

It's one thing to discipline yourself and show up with your willpower to work out and eat better, all in the name of taking care of your body for God. How different would it be if you chose to depend on God for every need of wisdom, strength and perseverance? I would venture to say that not only would it be different, it would be freeing.

Let's take it one step further. In regards to sin and areas of bondage, are you trying to overcome the desires of your flesh *with* God and His power? Or for God and by your strength? Committing to His way with Him includes the valleys.

A "With God" Testimony

I was once having a conversation with a sister I serve in our *Wellness His Way* community, who we will call Jess.[1] Jess shared this testimony with me that I'd like to share here, with her permission, of course. It reveals the "with" God journey of wellness, especially in the harder times.

Jess expressed that her greatest battle in her wellness journey seemed to always come back to nutrition, specifically snacking. She wanted to grow in her walk with God and learn how to do things with Him. As snack time approached, Jess prayed, "*God, I want to do this with You. I have an issue with snacking and just grabbing whatever. Please help me get through snack time and make choices that honor You."*

Afterward, she found some ice cream in her freezer with a serving left and proceeded to eat from the carton. Defeated, she prayed, *"God, what am I doing? Please help me!"* Suddenly, her husband called her on the phone (he was upstairs for a meeting) to tell her that he didn't have time to make a cup of coffee and wondered if she could do so for him. Though she was annoyed (because it interrupted her ice cream snack), she made him coffee and brought it upstairs. When she came back down, she realized that God had given her a way out of the temptation. She said to me, "This one moment with God empowered me to make better choices the whole week with Him, dependent on Him."

Experiencing Breakthrough with God

Jess' simple testimony reveals the beauty of walking with God in the big and in the small. It also illustrates the power and necessity of prayer to be strong in spirit and healthy in body. He sees it all and wants you to talk to Him and rely on Him through it all. It's truly beautiful how one conversation with God about our health (or anything) can change our direction. Imagine if we had many conversations with Him throughout the day!

A member of our community recently asked me how to press on with God when we don't see breakthroughs in the day-to-day. My response was in the form of two questions. First, "How do you define a breakthrough?" Second, "How does God define breakthrough according to His Word?"

When God asks things of us, His greatest desire is that we would do them with Him—*together*. If He is calling you to greater discipline with your health, He desires for you and Him to do it *together*. If He is revealing an idol in your life, He desires for you and Him to conquer it *together*. Define breakthrough with God. Write a vision for your health with Him. Then, start taking steps with Him, seeking Him, believing that He loves to speak and counsel you in the everyday things.

May today be the day you put an end to silence or resistance when it comes to talking with God about your health. I really believe that one open and honest conversation with God about your health could change everything. Consult and connect with your Creator, friend! He loves to hear your voice and make His way and Himself known to you.

With this in mind, as you set goals for your health, set goals that keep you relying on Him, close to Him, and enhance your walking with Him. Ask yourself, "How can I take a step *with* God *before* doing for God?" Start with God, stay with God, and end with God. Remaining in Him makes all the difference. I pray you discover the richness of God's presence in your everyday life and come to resist doing anything apart from Him!

PRAYER

Heavenly Father, I praise and glorify You! Thank you for Your promise to walk daily with me as I walk with You. Forgive me for my pride and for choosing my way instead of trusting Yours. I pray that today I would do all things with You, through Your power, and for Your glory. May I keep my heart soft to Your corrections if I lose my way and drift into doing things apart from You. In reality, apart from You I can do nothing of eternal value. I love You! Thank You for loving me first. Amen.

REFLECT

❶ What areas of your life are you finding you've been doing for God but not with Him?

....

....

....

....

....

....

....

....

....

....

....

❷ To which of the three ways of getting lost are you most susceptible? Your way for your gain, God's way for your gain, or your way for God's glory? What steps can you take to turn it to His way, with Him, and for His glory?

....

....

....

....

....

....

....

....

....

....

....

❸ How different would your wellness journey be if you committed to every part of it with God while abiding in Him?

....

....

....

....

....

....

....

....

....

....

....

....

GODFIDENCE >
CONFIDENCE

*D*o you really care about who God says you are? This may seem like a blunt question to kick us off, but I really want you to pause and answer this before reading on. You may know what He says about you, but do you *care*? Do you *believe* it? Do you *want to* believe who He says you are and live by His truth *more* than by what others say about you or what you think about yourself?

If your identity is not solidified in who you are in Christ, you'll keep looking for the significance you can only get from God everywhere else but Him. This guarantees a life of exhaustion, emptiness, and a constant state of brokenness.

STRONG IN SPIRIT

If we want to grow in Godfidence more than confidence, we must know the source of our Godfidence and define confidence.

The Source of Godfidence

Godfidence is a state of awareness of who we are in Christ, His promises and His power. Godfidence isn't just believing *in* God but also *believing* God. In comparison, Oxford Language defines confidence as a "feeling of self-assurance arising from one's appreciation of one's own abilities or qualities."[1] Can you already tell how self-sourced confidence is shaky ground, unreliable, and leaves us vulnerable?

What you think about yourself and what others think about you can change in a matter of minutes. But God? His Word is unchanging. His Word is absolute Truth; it's solid and permanent. Wouldn't you rather find your value, significance, worth and identity in Him? When our confidence comes from *who* we are in Christ and who *He* is, we become unshakable and can better resist the enemy's lies.

Identity Crisis

Identity is one of the primary places Satan likes to turn God's periods into question marks. The enemy comes to steal, kill and destroy, and he plants thoughts and ideas that leave us doubtful of our identity in Christ. One of the best examples of this is when Jesus was tempted by Satan in the wilderness just after He was baptized.

> *As soon as Jesus was baptized, he went up out of the water. At that moment heaven was opened, and he saw the Spirit of God descending like a dove and alighting on him. And a voice from heaven said, "This is my Son, whom I love; with him I am well pleased."*
>
> —Matthew 3:16–17

Then Jesus was led by the Spirit into the wilderness to be tempted by the devil. After fasting forty days and forty nights, he was hungry. The tempter came to him and said, "If you are the Son of God, tell these stones to become bread."

—Matthew 4:1–3

Where did Satan attack first? Identity. Right after God made it clear that Jesus was His Son whom He loved and with whom He was pleased, Satan came in and said to Jesus, "**If** you are the Son of God..." [emphasis added]. Jesus *knew* who He was and overcame Satan's temptations with absolute and permanent truth; the Word of God, aka the Sword of the Spirit. Jesus is our example, and His Spirit is in us and ready and able to give us that same Godfidence to stand firm in our identities in Christ! You will not be a victim to the enemy's lies when you know, believe and trust in the Truth!

Who God Is and Who He Says I Am

I would like to share with you two things I personally meditated on daily when I needed a major renewal in my mind regarding my identity in Christ: the attributes of God and who He says I am. These are things I still daily meditate on to this day, because my past thoughts and mindset can still creep up unannounced. I must be ready, and so must you!

Here are ten attributes of God (these are only some) that I invite you to meditate on:

1. God is *Infinite*—He is self-existing, without origin (Colossians 1:17).
2. God is *Immutable*—He never changes (Malachi 3:6).

3. God is *Omnipotent* and *Omniscient*—He is all-powerful and all-knowing (Psalm 33:6, Isaiah 46:9–10).
4. God is *Omnipresent*—He is always everywhere (Psalm 139:7–10, Psalm 137).
5. God is *Faithful*—He is infinitely true (Deuteronomy 7:9, 2 Timothy 2:13).
6. God is *Good*—He is infinitely kind and full of goodwill (Psalm 34:8).
7. God is *Merciful*—He is infinitely compassionate and kind (Romans 9:15–16).
8. God is *Gracious*—God is infinitely willing to spare the guilty (Psalm 145:8).
9. God is *Loving*—God infinitely loves us (1 John 4:7–8).
10. God is *Holy*—He is infinitely perfect (Revelation 4:8).

Which one did you need most as a reminder today? Again, these are just some. When we focus on who God is and work on believing He is who He says He is, it changes how we treat ourselves and engage with others.

In addition to knowing who God is, Godfidence is believing who God says *you* are in Him. You will find more peace in your health journey when your identity is rooted and established in Christ alone! Read the following promises and personalize them by inserting your name in the blank:

_____ , I know you by name (Isaiah 43:1).
_____ , You are My workmanship, created to do good works (Ephesians 2:10).
_____ , Your citizenship is in Heaven (2 Timothy 1:7).
_____ , You are a new creation (2 Corinthians 5:17).

_____ , You are fearfully and wonderfully made (Psalm 139:14).
_____ , I have loved you with an everlasting love (Jeremiah 31:3).
_____ , I gave my life for you (John 3:16).
_____ , I have great plans for you (Jeremiah 29:11).
_____ , Nothing can separate you from My love (Romans 8:38).
_____ , I will wipe every tear from your eye (Revelation 21:4).
_____ , I will strengthen you and help you (Isaiah 41:10).
_____ , I want you to have life and have it to the full (John 10:10).
_____ , I take great delight in you (Psalm 147:11).
_____ , I am with you everywhere you go (Matthew 28:20).
_____ , I will never leave you nor forsake you (Hebrews 13:5).

This is the source of our *God*fidence. God made us so we get our significance and security from Him alone. When we find it only in Him, we no longer idolize things and turn good things into god things. This includes our health!

HEALTHY IN BODY

Our health and wellness journey becomes complicated when we search for our identity and significance in it.

Misplaced Identity

For so many years, my confidence and identity were defined by my weight, size and calorie burn. As I've shared, this path led to total brokenness. Every attempt I made to get healthy while putting my identity into my health led to the same outcome: defeat, discouragement and discontentment. When I finally reached the end of my rope and asked the Holy Spirit to renew my mind, one of the first places He began was with *who* God really is and who I am in Him.

If you want to shift from confidence to Godfidence in your health, you must be willing to identify where you've been looking for significance and confidence outside of the Lord. Once you reveal this personal answer through an honest heart check, you can partner with the Holy Spirit to renew this misplaced identity.

Shaky Ground

How many times have you relied on the scale or the way your body looks to boost your confidence? It's true that when we *feel* good in our skin, we are more confident in our day-to-day interactions. The danger is that our confidence is reliant on a very unstable foundation.

The scale may say you're down one pound today but then up two pounds tomorrow. Your body may feel good today and then bloated tomorrow. You may be able to do twenty burpees today but then get injured and able to do none tomorrow. (Sorry to all who already hate burpees and may have been slightly traumatized by that example. I for one am the weird one who enjoys them, but push-ups are another story!)

You get my point. God made us in a way where our significance, value and identity can only be found in Him, our Creator. If we search for them anywhere else, or if something starts to influence us more than God does, it will become an idol. For example, the scale can be a useful tool...until we use it to define ourselves, our worth and our success. Food is nourishing and even pleasurable...

until we run to it for comfort, rather than to the Lord as our Comforter. Exercise is beneficial...until we tie our identity to the calories we've burned.

When our level of confidence is dependent on the things of this world, like what the scale says, how sweaty we get in our workout, or how well our jeans fit, we will be on a lifelong rollercoaster ride of insecurity and fear. Those are two things Jesus certainly did not die for.

Solid Ground

When our identities are sealed in Christ and we are content in Him (Godfidence), we can care for our bodies peacefully. Let me ask you, when was the last time you exercised or ate a meal from a place of security, Godfidence and joy? When our identities are no longer tied to our body image or diet culture rules, we can finally uncomplicate healthy living. We can finally just do the workout, eat healthily, savor the dessert, and move on!

The next time you notice your confidence shaken because of external circumstances with your health, pause and immediately meditate on the character of God and who you are in Him. Ask the Holy Spirit to help you *believe* those statements above as you memorize them and speak them over yourself often. Watch how everything else you do today (including taking care of your health) will be done with peace, joy and freedom!

PRAYER

Father, thank You for always being faithful and true, and for Your steadfast love which never ceases. Help me have confidence that You will always be there for me and will never leave or forsake me. Thank You for Your tender love for me. Help me stop placing my security, worth and identity in things like my body, career, finances or relationships. With this in mind, You tell me I can overcome the downward spiral of discontentment. Instead, may I only allow You to define me and not the things of this world or others. I am who You say I am. May Your truth wash over me and help me walk in godly confidence today. I love You! Amen.

REFLECT

❶ What do you usually rely on for confidence?

....
....
....
....
....
....
....
....
....
....

❷ Once something influences us more than God does, it's an idol. Has your health ever been an idol?

....
....
....
....
....
....
....
....
....
....
....
....
....

❸ Which of God's promises, which you've personalized by adding your name, resonates the most with you in this season?

....
....
....
....
....
....
....
....
....
....
....
....

PURPOSE > PREFERENCE

*R*emember the first time I heard the concept of choosing purpose over preference from Michelle Myers.[1] I had never realized how many times I was choosing my preferences, comfort and convenience over purpose in the day-to-day. Since then, it's something I often repeat in my mind, regardless of what I'm doing.

Having preferences is not wrong, but they are definitely "less than" because they are not what we are called to pursue. If we have opinions that compromise God's Word and purpose, we will be more likely to lose our way, because we will choose our way.

This chapter will invite you to reflect more than others. I encourage you to take this chapter slowly (maybe even over a day or two) and make time to prayerfully think about the questions I will invite you to ponder throughout!

STRONG IN SPIRIT

Do you care more about what you want for your life or what God wants for your life? If that question steps on your toes a bit, just know I got mine stepped on first! Yet, it's a good start to assess our true heart condition.

Our culture today is big on the pursuit of happiness, and this heavily influences our bent to choose our preferences over God's purpose. Yet God does not call us to a life of whatever makes us *happy*, but to a life of whatever makes us *holy* (1 Peter 1:14–16). When we are pursuing happiness apart from holiness, our preferences will always be the "greater" and the primary motivators of our decisions.

Another danger is the sense of entitlement our preferences can bring. We start to believe that obstacles, discomfort, inconveniences or suffering can't possibly be God's will. We think that if something makes us happy, it's the obvious right choice, and if it leaves us unhappy it's the wrong choice. Even more so, if our preferences are left unchecked and not submitted under God's authority, they can turn into idols when we pursue them more than God and His way.

His Purpose, His Way

"For my thoughts are not your thoughts, neither are your ways my ways," declares the LORD.

—Isaiah 55:8

Choosing purpose over preference starts with humbly remembering that God's way is not our way. His way is rarely comfortable, quick or convenient. His way *is* perfect because He is perfect, and His way perfects us by making us more like Him. When we deny ourselves, we also deny selfish preferences that hinder us from making much of Christ.

Trust in the Lord with all your heart and lean not on your own understanding; in all your ways submit to him, and he will make your paths straight.

—Proverbs 3:5–6

These verses remind us that in choosing God's way over our way, we must trust Him and His purpose, plan and will for our lives completely. Trust is vital to experiencing the amazing life God offers us in relationship with Him. The same way I can only trust my car to the extent that I believe it can get me somewhere safely, I can only trust people to the extent that I believe they are trustworthy.

God is perfectly trustworthy. We are loved and pursued by God, who *"...so loved the world, that he gave his only Son, that whoever believes in him should not perish but have eternal life"* (John 3:16). God has already given us everything we need to trust Him, His heart and His character. No matter how trustworthy God is, we must still make the decision to trust Him daily.

Proverbs 3:5–6 also reveals that we are not to lean on our own understanding. This doesn't mean we can't have understanding and use our brains. God gave us brains, and He wants us to use them! We must simply be aware that our understanding has human limits and is often influenced by our preferences, old thoughts and old self. This is why we are advised in 2 Corinthians 10:5 to take every thought captive and make it obedient under Christ.

Yielding to God's purpose and choosing His way involves submitting our own understandings and preferences under His authority. This act of submission doesn't have to be a *have to* (duty) but a *get to* (delight) when our trust is in God's holy sovereignty.

The Long Way Around

It is not unusual for God's purpose to take us in a direction we don't prefer, or that may not seem efficient to us. We see an example of this in Exodus 13:17–18, when God led the Israelites out of Egypt. *"When Pharaoh let the people go, God did not lead them on the road through the Philistine country, though that was shorter. For God said, 'If they face war, they might change their minds and return to Egypt.' So God led the people around by the desert road toward the Red Sea."*

God didn't choose the easier or shorter path. Instead, He intentionally took the Israelites the long way around. I'm sure they weren't too happy about it. After longing for freedom for around four hundred and thirty years, the last thing they would have preferred was "the long way around." God had their *needs* (purpose) in mind, not their *wants* (preference). The extra miles weren't a punishment but part of His provision and protection.

The Israelites' journey with God was long and full of ups and downs. When the journey became too long, they relied on their own understandings and preferences and turned to other gods to speed up the process (Exodus 32).

Aren't we often tempted to do the same? We can be quick to get frustrated with God when things aren't going our way or following our preferred timetable. In those moments, we must humble ourselves and remember God's purpose for us, which is to delight in Him, become more like Him, and magnify Him. Godly character grows most in suffering, valleys and the wilderness.

Suffering Has Purpose

God wastes nothing. God does not waste pain, suffering, waiting or seasons. Sometimes we question God's goodness and His way when it's filled with pain. Yet, when we trust that God is the One dictating our steps, we can have peace even in the midst of pain. Peace and pain can coexist because peace is not an emotion but a state of mind that is given to those who truly know God. As we keep our minds steadfast on the Lord and trust in His higher purpose, we can dwell in perfect peace (Isaiah 26:3).

Not only so, but we also glory in our sufferings, because we know that suffering produces perseverance; perseverance, character; and character, hope. And hope does not put us to shame, because God's love has been poured out into our hearts through the Holy Spirit, who has been given to us. —Romans 5:3–5

When things get hard, my bent is to run. Perseverance is not attractive. Yet, Romans reveals that when we glorify Him in our sufferings and refuse to prematurely uproot ourselves from hardship, we get to experience the fruit of perseverance: Christ-likeness. Suffering makes us more like Christ, which increases our glorifying Him in three ways:

1. Suffering often exposes idols in our lives, as well as hidden sins in our hearts in order to produce holiness (Philippians 1:8–11, 27; 2:14–15).

2. Suffering kills our pride so that humility can increase (Philippians 2:3–5).
3. Suffering allows us to receive God's comfort, which produces more compassion in us. This helps us point others to Him as the Comforter, as we also comfort others (2 Corinthians 1:3–5).

When we remember and trust God's purpose, we will not run from suffering or uproot ourselves prematurely from difficulties (our preferences) because we know He is working it all together for our eternal good and His glory in the end (Romans 8:28).

The Mundane Has Purpose

With that said, yielding to God's purpose isn't only reserved for the valley. We make countless decisions every single day and are in need of God's wisdom for each one. If you are not sure of God's purpose in an area of your life, you only need to ask for His wisdom!

When Christ comes to live in us and the Holy Spirit indwells us, He offers wisdom that is applicable to *every* decision we make. Not only is God's wisdom always a reflection of His purpose, but it's also not hidden from us. We grow in wisdom when we fill our hearts with His Word, which is His way. We are reminded in James 1:5 that if we lack wisdom, we just have to ask for it...because we are loved by a generous God!

As we unpack the practicality of choosing purpose over preferences in our day-to-day health decisions, my prayer is that you would first reflect on the question I started this chapter with: "Do you care more about what you want for your life or what God wants for your life?"

If the answer is God, rather than running from His way, resenting it or resisting it, may you rejoice in it! His purpose is, as Roman 8:28 promises us, always for the good of those who love Him!

HEALTHY IN BODY

Patient Endurance or Shortcut?

There are two things I invite you to reflect on today when it comes to choosing Purpose > Preference in your wellness journey. The first involves an awareness of your mindset and attitude when you're not seeing your definition of results fast enough in your health. When things aren't going your preferred way, are you more likely to quit? When it gets uncomfortable, do you try to find a shortcut?

I can't help but remember what the Israelites did in Exodus 32. A quick recap:

- Moses goes up the mountain to meet with God.
- The Israelites grow impatient.
- Rather than waiting patiently, they have another leader (Aaron) make them a golden calf to worship instead of God.

We do this too. I'll be the first to admit it! Maybe we don't build an actual cow of gold to worship, but how often do we create our own way when God's way is taking too long to either come to fruition or to even understand?

God often takes us the longer way *because* He loves us. It's because He loves us that He allows an environment that reveals the true condition of our hearts. This is so we can be transformed and His name alone can be glorified. We may not always understand His ways, but we can trust them because He is trustworthy. One of my favorite reminders I once heard in church is how all throughout Scripture we see that God is always effective, even when He doesn't seem to be efficient to us.

You may prefer the shortcut to weight loss. You may prefer a faster, easier and more convenient way. Are you willing to lay down that preference for His greater purpose for you in a slower journey? A journey that starts on the inside?

The next time you find yourself tempted to quit or take matters into your own hands, pray and ask the Holy Spirit to help you remain faithful. When we trust that God has our best interests in mind, we can live wholly for His glory and purpose.

Pursuing Wisdom in the Small

The second thing I want you to reflect on is the more lighthearted preferences that, if not checked, can make room for big hindrances in purpose. I once read an article by Melissa Dahl where she shares research that reveals how we make about two hundred decisions for our health each day. That honestly blew me away but also didn't surprise me! So many of our health decisions are made unconsciously. What if we asked for God's wisdom in each one? How would that impact our decision making?

The truth is, our selfish preferences appeal to our flesh. Sleeping in, skipping workouts, eating whatever, and neglecting this earthly "tent" are often the easier choices. It takes intention to lay down our preferences every day and make the next best, wise and right choice rather than the easy one.

Again, preferences here are the "less than." It's not wrong to have them. I prefer pecan pie over pumpkin pie. I also prefer early mornings over late evenings. These aren't hindering preferences because they don't impact our personal walk with God or our witness. It's when our selfish preferences compromise loving God with all our heart, loving our neighbor, or making Jesus known that we need to be most alert and willing to be redirected.

Many of our decisions can be filtered through the question, "Does my preference in this moment hinder me from delighting in the Lord and making Him known?" If you want to commit to taking care of your health with God *His* way and for *His* glory, it starts by remembering His purpose for you: to know Him intimately and to magnify Him in all you do, have, say and think.

A few challenges today:

- When you're tempted to hit snooze instead of spending time with the Lord, focus on what you want *most* over what you want in the moment.
- When you want to skip your workout, choose to focus on stewardship through movement rather than idleness.
- When you're scared to take a rest day, remember it's a chance to build your trust in the Lord as God of the outcome, rather than having to prove your worth or significance through performance or productivity.
- When you're tempted to overeat, run to God as your eternal refuge rather than food as a temporary relief.

The Holy Spirit in you is able to empower you to choose God's purpose with delight. You need only ask! As you do, I invite you to meditate on these five Scriptures as you remain steadfast in caring for the body you've been given:

1. You are a living sacrifice (Romans 12:1).
2. You do not run aimlessly (1 Corinthians 9:26–27).
3. Do it all for the glory of God (1 Corinthians 10:31).
4. You can do all things through His strength (Philippians 4:13).
5. Train for godliness (1 Timothy 4:8).

PRAYER

Jesus, You are the perfect example of choosing purpose over preference. In the Garden of Gethsemane, You expressed Your preference for the cup to be taken from You, but You also yielded to God's will and chose purpose. You chose our salvation over Your comfort. May I be a willing vessel ready to be used by You and joyfully yield to Your purpose and plans for me. I know my life is not my own; it is Yours to work through me. Lord, I am grateful for this life You've given me. Help me understand how to cultivate what You've given me with Your purpose in mind, including my body, to bring glory to Your great name. I love You. Amen!

REFLECT

❶ Do you care more about what you want for your life or what God wants for your life? Does the way you live match your answer?

....
....
....
....
....
....
....
....
....
....
....

❶ How have seasons of suffering grown your faith?

....
....
....
....
....
....
....
....
....
....
....
....
....

❶ In health, are you quick to quit or find a shortcut when things aren't going your way? How can choosing purpose help you persevere with God?

....
....
....
....
....
....
....
....
....
....
....
....
....
....

Faith > Fear

I'll be the first to admit that it's so easy to allow the cares of this world, others' opinions, and life circumstances to shift my gaze off the Lord. Fear can be a ferocious giant and, like a weed, can choke our faith.

I've seen that when I prioritize feeding my faith, fear is starved and not given room to derail me. There are, of course, healthy elements to fear, which is why it's "less than." Fear occurs when we see a threat and can be a helpful "alarm" when we are in need of a shift in direction. In this chapter, I am more specifically addressing faith-choking fear. The kind of fear that can brainwash us of God's promises, presence, faithfulness and goodness. This kind of fear can lead us into a downward spiral of poor decisions, disobedience and pride.

STRONG IN SPIRIT

Disarm Fear with Faith
Faith comes by hearing and hearing by the word of God.
—Romans 10:17 (English Standard Version)

We can disarm our fears with our faith. Charles Spurgeon defined faith as being made up of three components: *knowledge, belief and trust.*[1]

The more we spend time *knowing* God in His Word, the more our faith grows. When we rely on the Holy Spirit to lead us into all truth (John 16:13), our understanding and knowledge of God's Word grow.

With knowledge must come *belief.* It's one thing to know the Word; it's another thing to fully believe it. When we believe the truth of God's Word, we are able to receive it and allow it to transform our minds and hearts. As a therapist, I would often help my clients discover their core beliefs (which we will address more in chapter 13: *Beliefs > Behavior*). You see, when a trigger in life happens, it sparks a chain of thinking that is primarily influenced by our core beliefs. From there, our emotions follow and then our actions. Do you see now why your core beliefs matter so much? They are the funnel your thoughts come through.

Next comes *trust.* Ultimately, you can't put your trust in what you don't believe. There is a difference between believing what's in the Word of God and putting your trust in it. Trust is faith in *action.*

I've always loved the chair analogy to explain this. Let's say that you see a chair and you *know* it can support your weight and you also *believe* that it's safe to sit on. Despite knowing the chair can support your weight and believing it's safe to sit on, you refuse to sit on it. I would argue that your lack of trust to sit on the chair reveals your lack of true faith in the chair.

It is one idea to know and believe God, but it's another to trust Him, which fuels obedience. The more faith grows, the less fear chokes. We can grow our faith by spending intentional time in God's Word to study it, meditate on it, and memorize it. We can grow our faith by exercising it through our actions and allowing our deeds and obedience to reflect God's character and instruction. We can grow our faith by confessing what we believe, not what we feel. We can grow our faith by sharing it with others.

When we believe God is who He says He is, and we are who He says we are, we will not fall into the trap that comes from fear. When we know, believe and trust in His love, we can replace panic with prayer and make wise, faith-filled (instead of fear-filled) decisions that move us forward in His will.

The Fear of Man

There are many fears we can address, but perhaps the most subtle and enslaving is the fear of man.

> *Fear of man will prove to be a snare, but whoever trusts in the Lord is kept safe.*
> —Proverbs 29:25

The fear of man can manifest itself in several different ways, such as the need for approval, fear of disapproval, peer pressure, need for recognition, fear of criticism, fear of failure, fear of humiliation, fear of disappointing others, fear of falling behind, or the fear of missing out. These are just to name a few!

We obey what we fear, which is what makes the fear of man one of the most dangerous snares. If those fears lead, rather than the fear of the Lord, we can expect to stumble in disobedience, timidity, discouragement, inactivity, poor self-confidence, and instability in our faith. All those things not only choke our faith, they become roadblocks to serving and glorifying the Lord.

The fear of man sets us on the road to foolishness because it replaces the fear of the Lord, which is the beginning of all wisdom (Psalm 111:10). We are called to love and fear God supremely, which is what drives our obedience. Our obedience is interrupted and hindered when others' opinions and approvals become more important. Since fear can severely prevent us from having faith-filled obedience and doing God's will, we can see why the enemy works so hard to bring fear into our lives.

I've seen three consequences in my life that can result from the fear of man and would go as far to say that you have experienced some of these as well:

1. **Ineffectiveness:** We neglect God's calling for us when we fear man and are too preoccupied with what others are thinking. When we are constantly afraid of what people think, say, or can do to us, we spiritually stall. In other words, fear can immobilize us spiritually. Fear will also make God's Word unproductive in our lives. In describing the thorny ground, Matthew 13:22 reminds us that "the worries of this life and the deceitfulness of wealth choke it [the Word], making it unfruitful." God's Word can't bear fruit in us when we are actively walking in worry and fear.

2. **Idolatry:** Idolatry is present anytime we want anything more than Jesus and love anything more than Jesus. We can idolize things like others' opinions, the approval of others, and even the media's standard of health.

3. **Decision Paralysis:** We cannot move forward in the convictions and purpose God gives us when we are living out of fear. The fear of man can delay our obedience or even convince us that obeying partially is okay. When we are led by the Spirit and by the truth in God's Word, we make decisions with confidence, faith and wisdom.

While we fall into a trap when we are led by the fear of man, we are kept safe when we trust in the Lord. Trusting God is safe because He is the real God. That doesn't mean we will never feel afraid when obeying God. Sometimes we will feel a bit afraid! But let's not allow our fear to compromise our obedience. When we choose to obey, even if we feel afraid, we learn to trust God's promises more than our perceptions and reach the place where we can confidently say, *"The Lord is my helper; I will not fear; what can man do to me?"* (Hebrews 13:6).

But here's the thing: you won't trust the Lord if you don't truly know Him and believe Him. John 17:3 says, *"Now this is eternal life: that they know you, the only true God, and Jesus Christ, whom you have sent."* Knowing God on a personal and intimate level is more than head knowledge. It's fully accepting and receiving the promise of Jesus's sacrifice on the cross. We come to know God personally and intimately when we receive His free gift of salvation through faith in Christ Jesus, not by our own efforts or works (Ephesians 2:8–9).

The more you know, believe and trust in who God is, who He says you are, and His promises, the less you will be swayed by the fear of man.

The Three As

If you are battling the fear of man, I want to give you three "A"s to help you overcome this snare:

1. **Admit:** Confession restores your fellowship with God. When you recognize that anything has become more important than God, including others' opinions, you must confess it as a sin and repent of it. When you confess, you can be confident of God's immeasurable grace that picks you up and empowers you to make the next right choice with Him, through Him, and for His glory (1 John 1:9).

2. **Acknowledge:** Take time to consider the root of the fear you have. When you make time to articulate your fears, you can see that they are not bigger than God. You are able to find a promise in God's Word that disarms the fear and build a prayer around it (2 Corinthians 1:20).

3. **Attack:** Now that you've admitted (confessed) and acknowledged (assessed) the fear of man, you can attack and confront this giant head-on with faith and be fully confident of God's love, which casts out all fear (1 John 4:18). Exercise your faith (knowledge, belief, trust) in God by disarming the root of your fears with His Word, His promises, and His presence (Ephesians 6:17). Ask the Holy Spirit to increase your delight in the Lord that you may release all other forms of satisfaction.

Never forget that God's perfect love drives, pushes and casts away all of our fears. The next time you are tempted to let fear steer, I encourage you to pause and meditate on God's character, attributes and promises. I am confident that this will change the next choice you make.

HEALTHY IN BODY

With an understanding of how to fuel our faith and starve our fears (specifically the fear of man), let's identify practical ways to overcome fear with faith in our wellness journey.

I have seen how many times the fear of man has influenced my wellness decisions for the worse. I've learned that fear grows as pride grows. The more we believe success in our health is up to us, or we look all around (comparison) instead of *up*, we stumble. But when we place trust in the Lord and He is our gaze, we are kept safe. We are on a firm foundation.

There are three specific fears I'd like to highlight that can hinder our commitment to *Wellness His Way*.

The Fear of Missing Out

The fear of missing out is often driven by both pressure and comparison. Let's unpack them both together.

Pressure
It seems like there's always a new way to eat or a new way to exercise, and if you don't try it, you'll miss out or fall behind.

Something to ponder: How often do you make wellness decisions because of pressure? (It could be pressure you place on yourself or pressure that comes from the outside.)

I have seen how pressure increases the more we try to chase Jesus *and* the world. We want Jesus, but we also want to keep up with what the world is doing. We chase Jesus *and* the world when we try to be content in Christ *and* chase after shortcuts to achieve "*this* or *that*" body image. We chase Jesus *and* the world when we say Jesus is enough *and* obsess over the body image the world deems attractive. Do you feel the pressure yet?

We were never meant to run two races. We can't. Will you join me in choosing the "Jesus *only*" race today? When our identity is fully secure in Christ, we can exercise and nourish our bodies from a place of rest, because we rest in Christ. When our contentment is in Christ alone, we are better able to discern which wellness paths allow us to honor God with our bodies and which ones can lead to danger.

One of my trainers from my workout programs once said that we should ask ourselves if certain exercise is depleting us or energizing us. That has stuck with me and has helped me evaluate which workouts I engage in with more freedom!

Not to mention that there have been countless times where missing out was actually a joy and a wise choice! I remember when a fitness program came out that all my friends were excited to do. I checked out the sample workout and right away knew that the structure, trainer's style and intensity of the workouts would leave me depleted. This program would hinder me and not help me. So I confidently and joyfully chose to miss out.

There's another type of pressure as well, the kind that leaves us terrified of disappointing others. The kind of pressure that leaves us worried when we go to dinner parties or out to eat because we don't know how to say, "No, thank you!" Not everyone in your life will want to uplift you in your journey of wellness with God. Some won't understand it. Some will resent it. Some will test it. Some may even try to sabotage it.

If you have feared disappointing others so much that their opinions and judgments have become a louder voice than the voice of Truth, I encourage you to lean into the next few thoughts: What if loving others was more about being honest with your loved ones than it was about doing whatever it takes to please them? Lysa TerKeurst says it so well in her book *The Best Yes*: "We must not confuse the command to love with the disease to please." I love this differentiation between people-loving and people-pleasing!

Pleasing people leaves us powerless, voiceless and dishonest. In the end, we do not love well because truth is compromised. Even worse, we become quick to say yes to everyone at the cost of saying yes to the Lord. On the other hand, when we aim to love rather than please, we prioritize honesty and God's voice can lead. Let's live out 2 Corinthians 5:9: *"So whether we are at home or away, we make it our aim to please him."*

Comparison
Comparison is another seed that can grow in this fear. We are often too busy comparing our lives to the world instead of the Word. Comparison can be positive if we use it to recognize examples of godly characteristics in others that bring us closer to Jesus. Comparison becomes a thief of joy when we make the world and others around us our measuring sticks instead of God's Word.

I see comparison as a symptom of discontentment. When we are discontented with ourselves, our bodies, or our weight loss progress, we start to compare our race to others. Then we become weary in doing good when we see others succeeding faster than we are. We begin to wonder if we are falling behind and missing out *because* God is holding out on us or because we aren't doing more. Yet, God doesn't promise our definitions of success but *His*. As we talked about in an earlier chapter, He evaluates success by obedience and faithfulness to what He's called us to do, not by results.

With that in mind, what if we focus on obedience in caring wisely for our bodies rather than allowing comparison to lead us to reckless striving or hopeless quitting? What if, instead of comparing our bodies or wellness results to the person next to us, we made time to celebrate how God made us different? What if we spent more time focusing on whose image we are made in instead of all the images we aren't measuring up to? The more we are satisfied with Christ, the less we will fear missing out. Instead, we can use that energy to cheer on the people next to us as they commit to faithfulness in their unique races.

The Fear of Failure

Failure is inevitable. With that said, I must tell you that over the years, I have *learned* the value of seeing failure as necessary for the refinement of my soul and skills. It is therefore an ally, not an enemy. The belief that mistakes can be lessons and failure can be an ally didn't just happen. I had to make a conscious choice to see what I gained from failure rather than what I lost.

Failure can be a friend because it:

- Keeps us humble
- Gives us feedback (When you know better, you do better!)
- Can build our character (perseverance, patience, discipline)
- Reminds us of the need for grace
- Can reveal unrealistic expectations
- Allows us to course-correct
- Can move us into the next season of growth
- Keeps us teachable
- Teaches us what success can't

The key to failure is to stop identifying ourselves by our events. Just because you failed doesn't mean you are a failure. You are not defined by your struggles! Let's learn how to run to Jesus when we fail, instead of away from Him, and not give our struggles more power than they have. Instead, claim who you *really* are in Christ: His child!

If you've struggled with overeating today, know that God's grace is near and accessible to you. Be willing to study your triggers and ask the Lord to help you, as well as seek out accountability from others.

If it's been a week or more since you've intentionally exercised, make the decision right now to recommit to discipline and find a routine that can lead to consistency, not just short bursts of intensity.

If your body is feeling more fatigued and you can't perform in your workouts as well as earlier this week, choose the pace of grace your body needs, instead of setting it up for failure with unrealistic expectations.

If you're quick to give up when things get hard or uncomfortable, first ask the Lord for strength. Then make it your goal to finish the workouts you start, even if it means you modify or take a lot of breaks. This will build perseverance and endurance. Reframe modifying when needed as a way to steward your body well and be kind toward where it is today!

May you never forget that God is bigger than your failure! What I love is that all throughout Scripture, we see how the Kingdom of God was intentionally built by those who learned how to fail forward by clinging to grace and being fueled by faith. Let's do the same!

The Fear of Success

This may seem like an odd one, but I find it to be one reason for self-sabotage, so I wanted to mention it briefly.

> *The horse is made ready for the day of battle, but victory rests with the LORD.*
> —Proverbs 21:31

This verse shows us that we do not need to fear success when God is the One giving it. Remember, the outcome is God's job, and obedience is ours. If God chooses to grant success for our faithfulness, let us be quick to give Him all the glory. One way we give Him glory is by continuing to rely on Him. Sometimes when we see success, we can get prideful. We try to see what we can get away with and still succeed. Protect yourself from this mindset by choosing humility and glorifying God instead of yourself in the success.

If you're seeing weight loss, praise God and write down what's working, focusing on how you're achieving health for your body more than a number on the scale.

If you said "no" to a food temptation you generally struggle with, praise God and trust that with His power, you can do it again. You will go further relying on His power than your willpower.

If you're no longer winded chasing your kids or going up the stairs, praise God for how your body is no longer hindering your daily functioning!

Again, the only time we should be concerned about success is if we're trying to achieve it our way, apart from God, and if in our success, we start to glorify ourselves instead of God.

If you abide in my word, you are truly my disciples, and you will know the truth, and the truth will set you free. —John 8:31–32

Jesus gives us the key that when we know the truth, we are set free from the fears and lies that keep us in chains. Disarm the fears we've covered today (and the others you wrestle with) with faith and with the Truth. If you'd like an extra challenge, I'd love to invite you to make a list of your top fears on one side of a sheet of paper and, on the other, disarm the fear with God's Word. In order to confront the lie, you must be aware of it. Therefore, take time to assess the fears that have been holding you back and choking your faith, trusting that you can overcome those fears by declaring God's promises and confessing what you believe (faith) and not what you feel (fear).

PRAYER

Jesus, thank You for Your perfect love that casts out all fear, that I am kept safe when I put my trust in You. There is no room for fear in Your love. Help me to feed my faith with Your Word, Your promises, and Your Truth so that the fears in this world have no hold on me. When fear creeps in and tells me I am not able, help me remember that You are able and I simply need to be available. Forgive me when I allow fear of man to influence me more than You. May the only fear I have be fearing You, that I may honor You and glorify You. I love You! Amen.

REFLECT

❶ Faith grows when we know, believe and trust God. Are you growing in all three areas? Is there one that needs more of your effort and God's power?

....

....

....

....

....

....

....

....

....

....

❷ How has the fear of man been a snare in your life?

....
....
....
....
....
....
....
....
....
....
....
....
....

❸ How can you start seeing failure as a friend, specifically in your health journey, and allow it to refine you rather than define you?

....
....
....
....
....
....
....
....
....
....
....
....

Growth Focused >
Goal Focused

*L*et me start this chapter by clarifying that I am not against goal setting. Since "maintenance mode" and comfort zones are a real temptation, goals can help sharpen our aim and enhance our ability to redeem time, talents, treasures, and even our temples well. Goals can help the passive person become proactive, but can lead the ambitious person down a path of greater striving (unless the goals are specific to rest and surrender).

Like anything that is good, our own goals can become idols if they influence and lead us more than Jesus and His Holy Spirit. We must be cautious to never desire the outcome of our goals more than Christ Himself.

STRONG IN SPIRIT

Delight Before Desire
Take delight in the Lord, and he will give you the desires of your heart.

—Psalm 37:4

I love to come back to this psalm to address the topic of goal-setting. Oftentimes we are quick to focus on the second half of this verse where God gives us the desires of our hearts, but miss the first half where we are to delight in Him. Delighting in the Lord is our highest purpose next to magnifying Him. He is to be the primary focus; everything else, every other goal, is secondary!

David's order shows us that delight comes before desires. The more we desire to grow in our delight for the Lord, the more we ask for desires that are according to His will and purpose and not our own. When we are delighting in the Lord, we desire what pleases and honors Him!

What is beautiful is that God never gives a commandment without also providing the enablement. So how do we awaken a desire to delight and rejoice in the Lord? We can't, but God can!

The Holy Spirit stirs this desire in our hearts and gives us the supernatural power to delight in the Lord. In Philippians 2:13, Paul commands us to work out our salvation and reminds us that it's God who works in us to will and act in order to fulfill His good purpose. As A.W. Tozer says in his incredible book *The Pursuit of God*, "We pursue God because, and only because, He has first put an urge within us that spurs us to the pursuit (and) when the Holy Spirit shows us God as He is, we admire Him to the point of wonder and delight."[1]

The word *delight* is a verb, which means it requires action. It's proactive, not passive. To delight in the Lord is to desire to be in His presence, to be near Him and hear His voice. The more we are in the presence of God and in prayerful communion with Him, the more the Holy Spirit transforms our hearts. The product of this is that our desires become His desires, and it is those desires He will grant. God will give us everything we need to glorify Him and do His will. The more God has our hearts, the more He trusts us with His blessings.

Make God the Goal

We set goals based on what we desire and want to see grow. When we want to be more productive in the mornings, we set a goal to wake up earlier and go to bed earlier. When we want to lose weight, we set the goal to work out more and eat better. We make time for what we deem a priority.

What would happen if we made God our goal and our highest priority? What if our greatest desire in terms of growth was to grow in knowing Jesus, delighting in Jesus, and glorifying Jesus? We won't always get this right, but it's certainly what we should aim most for.

When Christ is our goal, we pursue the things that keep us near Him and like Him. With this in mind, there are three questions I like to ask myself while I am setting goals:

1. Did I first seek the Lord and receive His peace regarding this goal?
2. What is the motivation behind the goal? Is it to please me or to glorify the Lord?
3. Am I fully surrendered to God's leading and holding loosely to the outcome?

When we are pursuing growth in the things that make us more like Christ, we are less derailed by our own pride. These questions can keep us humble and keep our minds on things above, not earthly things. We don't want to get lost in the strategic striving and pressure that goal-setting can bring.

Growth Takes God's Power and Our Efforts

Perhaps you are already starting to feel the tug to shift some things around and make Christ your primary aim. Perhaps you already recognize where your heart may be misaligned, preventing growth, and you're ready to fix it. To all my achievers and doers out there, may I remind you that when it comes to your sanctification and transformation, you need not strive. Instead, I find the best posture is to be still and willing, stand firm, and let God do the work in us. Any growth we achieve on our own results in external change without an internal transformation. God alone has the power to sanctify and change us into His likeness.

In his book *The Discipline of Grace: God's Role and Our Role in the Pursuit of Holiness*, Jerry Bridges says, "We try to change ourselves. We take what we think are the tools of spiritual transformation into our own hands and try to sculpt ourselves into robust Christlike specimens. But spiritual transformation is primarily the work of the Holy Spirit. He is the Master Sculptor. Grace and the personal discipline required to pursue holiness, however, are not opposed to one another. In fact, they go hand in hand. An understanding of how grace and personal, vigorous effort work together is essential for a life-long pursuit of holiness."

If I could sum up what Bridges is saying, it would be this: Spiritual growth is a work that God does in us, but it requires our effort and willingness. It also doesn't happen overnight. God rarely tackles all areas that need growth all at once. Instead, He slowly chisels the worldly parts while pruning the areas that do bear fruit. Why? So that they can bear more fruit. Our part is to come to the end of ourselves and surrender to Him. As we do, God works to accomplish His purpose in our lives.

Growth Takes Time

My favorite example of this comes from the life of Moses in the Old Testament. When I came to Deuteronomy 33–34 and the end of Moses's life, I noticed he was one hundred and twenty years old when he died. I am no math expert (for real, praise God for tutors), but I noticed that forty was a significant number in his life. Forty years as a prince of Egypt, forty years a shepherd in the wilderness, forty years leading Israel to the Promised Land.

Did you notice the first eighty years?! All prep. I am the woman who is constantly struggling with the waiting and preparation period. If Moses was willing to let God prepare him for eighty years for the last third of his life, we can learn to enjoy the preparation period too. God purposefully led Moses on a journey of slow growth to ensure he could withstand the trials the final third of his life would bring.

It's okay to grow slow, and just because you're struggling doesn't mean you're failing. Growth takes time. God takes His time, and friend, He is never late.

HEALTHY IN BODY

In our health, let's aim to set goals that honor God, strengthen our bodies, keep us reliant on Jesus, and enhance our ability to serve others.

The Growth That Matters Most

There have been seasons where all I cared about was the goal of losing weight, reaching a specific number on the scale, or fitting into a certain size. I neglected the non-scale victories and refused to see any kind of progress as meaningful if it wasn't *calculable*. More often than not, the growth that matters most can't be calculated by human standards.

In her book *Made To Crave*, Lysa TerKeurst writes, "The more I made exercise about spiritual growth and discipline, the less I focused on the weight."[3] I love this mindset shift! I remember when I was only goal focused, not seeing the scale move would lead me to think I was a failure and leave me minimizing all my efforts as meaningless. I would then be vulnerable to self-sabotage and extremes. When I began focusing on intentional growth, I was able to look past the scale and assess how I'd been growing in obedience, faithfulness, and surrender—what God cares about more.

In the end, the physical fruit that comes out of your effort and obedience is to be secondary. Calculable measures have their place and are not wrong to have. However, I am speaking to the person right now who has made the calculable measures more important than God's Word. Rather than only relying on calculable results as evidence of your progress, what if you started asking soul evaluation questions each week like:

- Did I run to God instead of ___?
- Did I honor God with my body?
- Am I closer to Jesus?
- Did I struggle less with pleasing my flesh?
- Did I faithfully steward the body I've been given?

Weight loss and inches lost are not wrong goals to set, but if they are our only focus, we will be left with the temptation to either strive when we see results or prematurely quit when we don't. When we are growth focused, we are able to persevere, which builds our character to be more like Christ!

Reach or Rest?

When it comes to goal-setting, I have discovered that just because something may benefit from progress or greater intention doesn't mean that it must become a goal in this specific moment. One of the things I have had to learn, for example, is that just because there is weight to lose doesn't mean weight loss needs to be a goal in this season.

There is a time to grow by setting goals that help us reach for more, and there is a time to grow by resting and doing less. Growth can look like periods of intense discipline *and* periods of intentional rest. This isn't a license for complacency or mediocrity. We can both reach and rest with excellence. Rest can mean maintaining progress and spending more time evaluating the condition of our heart and mind until we receive God's peace to reach for the discipline that prunes to bring more growth. Maintenance mode (weight-wise) is not failure, weakness or less than. It requires just as much intentionality, the same way rest does.

If you are in a season where a lot is changing, unpredictable and limited, right now may not be the wisest time to also add on weight loss as a goal. You can focus on purposeful movement, nourishment, rest and hydration without attaching a specific goal to it. When it's time to add the aim of something more specific, you will be able to add it with peace, not pressure.

Perhaps you're experiencing the opposite. Maybe you've been resting, but now the rest has turned into mediocrity or laziness and you know it's time to reach and elevate discipline. Here are some steps you can take if that's you:

1. Reflect on the long-term vision you have for your health, so you can identify a short-term goal or two that will help you get there. For example, if a long-term vision is strength, one goal you can set is strength training two to three times per week.

2. Make sure the goals you set will enhance you mentally, spiritually and emotionally in addition to physically. Sometimes we set goals that we can physically do but leave us mentally, spiritually or emotionally depleted.

3. Focus on one habit change at a time. Too many goals after a period of rest or less intensity will likely lead to overwhelm or discouragement.

4. Grab a friend and embrace accountability. Share your goal out loud with a friend or two, why you're reaching for it, and how you intend on pursuing it.

Have there been goals that may have been hastily pursued or prematurely set in your life? I encourage you to sit and talk with the Lord. Ask Him to give you His eyes and wisdom for your next step with this, and I am confident He will!

Grow Beyond the Goal

In summary, goal-focused people are often focused most on destination, stop when the goal is reached, and rely on motivation. Growth-focused people focus most on the journey, keep growing beyond the goal, and *practice* discipline.

When we are only goal focused, we may see a lot of results on the outside with little transformation on the inside. When we are growth focused, life is progressing on the outside *because of* the transformation God is doing on the inside.

Take time to reassess your goals and lay them at the feet of Jesus. If the goal helps sharpen your aim and keeps you proactive and productive in the things that matter most, keep it! If the goal is one that can shift your gaze off Christ, I encourage you to reconsider it.

It's God who ultimately brings the growth. God is the great supplier behind and in whatever actions we take as a means of His grace. So as you grow, make sure the praise goes back to Him!

Ultimately, may your greatest desire be to grow in your relationship with the Lord and in spiritual maturity. Partner with the Holy Spirit in the *heart* work, and He will help you do the hard work. Choose *Growth Focused > Goal Focused* and keep moving forward reliant on His grace.

PRAYER

Father, my greatest desire today is to taste Your goodness, fall more in love with You, and never forget that You alone are the God of the Harvest (Matt 9:38). It is by Your grace that growth happens. I also know that my showing up matters, so I pray that today I show up to steward what You've given me with purpose, joy and gratitude. I dedicate every aspect of my efforts today to You. I want Your goals to be my goals and Your purposes mine. Give me a teachable spirit so I can constantly increase the skills You have given me to honor You and bring You glory. I love You! Amen.

REFLECT

❶ Are you more goal focused or growth focused?

....
....
....
....
....
....
....
....
....
....
....

❷ We can be quick to want the desires of our hearts without first delighting in the Lord and asking the Holy Spirit to change our desires. How can you pursue greater delight in the Lord?

....
....
....
....
....
....
....
....
....
....
....

❸ Take time to reassess your goals and lay them at the feet of Jesus. Again, if the goal helps sharpen your aim and keeps you proactive and productive in the things that matter most, keep it! If the goal is one that can hinder you and shift your gaze off Christ, I encourage you to reconsider it.

....
....
....
....
....
....
....
....
....
....
....
....
....

HUMILITY > PRIDE

I must admit, writing this chapter was very humbling (see what I did there?). In the few weeks I've been working on it, the Holy Spirit has been doing major work in my heart around this subject. You see, pride is an area of my life that is not dead, which leaves me feeling unqualified to write about humility. But God. In His kindness and love, He reminded me that this book is not meant to be filled with my advice but with His Word, wisdom and direction. It's not meant to be a showcase of my skill but His spirit.

I am coming to you as a sister still fighting this ferocious and persistent giant in my life by the power of God. Right now you have an opportunity to practice humility by approaching this chapter with a humble heart, ready to receive heart checks, course corrections and mind redirections.

We cannot magnify Christ and be effective for the Kingdom if we are self-focused, self-centered and self-sufficient. Pride is something we will have to actively fight daily to kill. The good news, however, is that we can stand up to fight this daily battle against our pride, knowing that Christ has won the war. We can fight knowing His grace is sufficient and that the Holy Spirit is able to help us defeat pride when we take on the image of Christ and His humility.

STRONG IN SPIRIT

Committing to *Wellness His Way* means we depend on *Him,* not ourselves. Pride's greatest desire is to have its own way rather than His way. Trusting in God *is* the opposite of pride. Pride begs us to believe it all depends on us. Trusting God requires us to place our dependence on Him.

> *"He guides the humble in what is right and teaches them his way."*
>
> —Psalms 25:9

God teaches His way to the humble. If we want to learn, love and follow God's way, the starting point is humility. Humbling ourselves. Reaching the end of ourselves. Acknowledging that I'm the sheep and God is the Shepherd. We cannot like David declare that the Lord is our Shepherd (in Psalm 23) without first seeing that we are the sheep. To do this, we must also recognize where pride might be reigning in our hearts.

Pride's Threat

Ultimately, pride leaves us confident in our own abilities rather than reliant on God's grace. Pride can manifest itself in many different ways. It almost always leads to an incorrect view of God, an incorrect view of ourselves, and a reliance on ourselves as the solution or for satisfaction. I also find that we are more likely to focus on the arrogant side of pride when the insecure side of pride is just as dangerous.

Pride leaves us seeing ourselves as greater than we are or less than who we are in Christ. Pride leads us to measure our lives by the standard of our accomplishments or possessions rather than our God-given identities. Pride redirects our worship to ourselves instead of the Lord.

Our best example of pride in the Bible is Satan. Our best example of humility in the Bible is Jesus. We can learn from both, but are to only imitate the One—Jesus.

Satan is good at planting lies in our minds because he knows that once we believe something, that belief influences our behavior. Lies that can fuel pride include (but are not limited to):

- Thinking we are humble enough
- Choosing our comfort over others' (even worse, over others' souls)
- Thinking God doesn't care about what we do
- Thinking our sin is not too serious
- Thinking we are entitled to something
- Thinking we know what's best more than God does

Truth's Power
The only way to counter these lies is with the Truth. In order to kill the pride in us, we must commit to five principles:

Know God
Have you paused recently to meditate on who God is? I find we can be quick to thank God for what He's done, but how often do we adore Him for who He is? How often do we stop to consider His holiness? His infinite wisdom? His never-ending glory? His faithfulness? His sovereignty in working all things out according to the counsel of His will? How majestic He is and yet how much He cares about every detail of our lives? His goodness?

I love this quote by Brian Hedges: "The great secret to humility is not to focus on yourself at all, but to fill your mind and heart with the glory of God revealed in the sin–conquering death and resurrection of Jesus Christ."[1] Pride kicks in when we have a view or understanding of God that is lower than ourselves. We must intentionally increase Him in our lives and decrease our own opinion of ourselves.

Know Yourself

Friend, you and I are the receivers of God's immeasurable grace and goodness. In Ephesians 2:1–3, we see we were hopeless, helpless, and living according to this world. We were following Satan and living to satisfy our desires. But God. He displayed the riches of His grace and gave us life. Pride has absolutely no room, not even in our good works. Ephesians 2:10 reminds us that we are God's handiwork, created in Christ Jesus to do good works. This means that God is not even surprised when we do good. He planned it! He alone is to get all the glory every time.

Follow Jesus's Example

Jesus is the ultimate example of humility, and we are commanded to follow His example (Philippians 2:5–8). Though Jesus was equal with God, He took upon Himself a human nature and took on our likeness. He humbled himself and was obedient till death. God-pleasing obedience is paved with humility. Remember Jesus when you're struggling to pursue and choose humility. His Spirit is in you, helping you live as He did.

Ask for and Pursue Humility

God's desire for us is our sanctification and for us to be holy, as He is holy. He is the One who brings holiness to fruition. We must be dependent on the Holy Spirit to live in humility. But please hear me; it's not enough to just pray for humility. We must also actively pursue it. How? We pursue humility by daily surrendering our wants, needs, and desires at Jesus's feet. We pursue humility by daily preaching the gospel message to our soul. We pursue humility by coming to a point where we actually hate and grieve our pride. We pursue humility by thinking of ourselves less.

The more we intentionally remember the gospel message, the less pride can brainwash us of it. The more we focus on what Jesus has done, the less we can boast about anything we can do. The more we grow in humility, the more we can be used by God for His Kingdom. I love how Max Lucado puts it: "Those who walk in pride, God is able to humble. But those who walk in humility, God is able to use."[2]

Meditate on God's Word
Meditating daily on God's Word is the key to it all. We are reminded in 2 Timothy 3:16–17 that all Scripture is inspired by God and is profitable for teaching, rebuking, correcting and training in righteousness so that we may be complete and equipped for every good work.

If you want to deepen your understanding of the truth about God, search His Word. If you want to know the truth about yourself, search His Word. If you want to follow Christ's example, search His Word. When you read His Word, believe it, live it, and you will be sanctified day by day!

We ultimately cannot live for God's glory apart from true humility. True humility is acknowledging God as the giver of everything we have and acting on that knowledge by living for God's glory alone. True humility doesn't mean we never accept kind words or compliments from others. What humility does is keep us grounded in who we boast in when we do get the compliments. For example, humility can respond in this way: "Thank you for your kind words! I wouldn't have been able to do this without God. It was by His grace and for His glory!" You can thank others for their kind words *while* pointing them to Jesus! We are made to live a life of effective and good work. We must simply remember that every good and perfect gift comes from above (James 1:17).

HEALTHY IN BODY

For some of us, our wellness journey may be an area where pride reigns. I shared before that God can absolutely use our wellness journey, but so can Satan. Satan's favorite way to turn a good thing into a god thing is to have us think we don't need God and that we deserve to do things our way, for our gain and for our glory.

I have witnessed and lived the side of pride that is quick to tell God "I got this" instead of "I need You." Pride leads us to believe we know the right way. Even worse, we are offended and angry with God when He does not agree with our way! Every time we choose our way, it leads to greater bondage and despair. This should be no surprise to us since Proverbs 16:18 clearly warns us that pride goes before destruction.

The Three Traps of Pride

In order to pursue humility in our wellness journey, we must be aware of where pride can grow. Here are three possible traps:

Pride glorifies itself
Yet, God reminds us that every good thing comes from Him (James 1:16–17). With that in mind, when you experience success in your wellness journey, be careful not to glorify the weight loss, yourself (including your own image), or the success. All glory belongs to God alone. It is wise to also be careful of glorifying oneself in comparison to others. For example: "Wow, I have made a lot of progress compared to that person." Make an effort to purposefully look for ways to give God glory in the big and small moments of your wellness journey. Pride has little room to grow when you're in a consistent posture of humility and praise.

Pride loves self-promotion
Do you work out to be seen by others? To be noticed? To be complimented? Does praise humble you or intensify your craving for more? It's not wrong to receive a compliment, but we are on shaky ground if we do it *for* the compliment. Matthew 6:1 cautions us, *"Be careful not to practice your righteousness in front of others to be seen by them. If you do, you will have no reward from your Father in heaven."*

We are wired to appreciate and even long for affirmation from others. The danger is that affirmation from others can become what we desire more than God and His *"Well done, good and faithful servant."* (Matthew 25:23)

Not every workout, meal, or victory needs to be shared publicly. When you do share, just do a quick heart check to get to the motive behind the sharing. For example: When you share, are you constantly checking for likes, recognition and the fire emoji? Do you often hope someone will make a comment on how great you look? Do you choose your workout clothes based on what will likely get the most attention?

If this is an area of real struggle, an idea might be to take a short period of time to continue remaining faithful in your wellness journey without sharing every detail out loud. This may not be necessary for everyone, but I trust the Holy Spirit will make it known if it's the right step for you.

Pride can be low self-esteem and self-degradation
We don't expect to find pride in our hearts when we are failing, but it's just as much of a temptation in failure as it is in success. When we tear ourselves down, there is still a preoccupation with self. Pride then manifests itself as low self-esteem, and the desire to be great subtly fuels it.

A great danger of low self-esteem is discouragement. In Exodus 6:9, God declares all His promises to the Israelites as He prepares to free them from slavery in Egypt. When Moses goes to relay the message of hope, the Israelites *"did not listen to him because of their discouragement and harsh labor."*

One of the most subtle traps of discouragement is that it leaves us talking more than listening. Rather than listening to who God says we are, the soundtrack of our minds is filled with negative self-talk and hopelessness. For example: "I keep overeating. I can't get anything right. I'll never break this habit. Why can't I be like other people who don't struggle with this? Why bother caring anymore?"

As we can see, not only does a low view of self still leave us absorbed with ourselves, it also leaves us deaf to God's encouragement. If this is the battle you're facing today, I encourage you to preach God's Word to your soul out loud. Right now say, "Enough! God, please help me quiet my soul so I can hear Your voice. Remind me who You are and who I am in You."

Distraction from the Main Thing

Satan loves to distract. If he can keep us distracted and absorbed with ourselves, we will neglect our primary purpose, which is the gospel. Really think about this with me. Our purpose is to delight in the Lord, exalt Him as we go, make disciples, and spread the gospel to all nations. Jesus never said that our commission was to go out and be *this* weight, *that* size, or have a six-pack!

I remember when I was in the midst of my food addiction. As a youth leader, I dreaded going to youth events for fear of the food that would be there. When I would go, my mind would be more consumed with the "what ifs" of making a poor food choice than the conversations and souls I was there to love and point to Jesus. I thought avoiding church events was a healthy boundary for my body when in reality, it was compromising my ministry.

Sometimes what hinders us from loving God and loving people isn't obvious rebellion but subtle distraction. The moment we make our bodies the main thing, we lose sight of God's purpose and way. Our bodies aren't the main thing. *We* aren't the main thing. We are God's creations, and we exist to display and magnify God's glory. In the same way, our bodies are vehicles for His glory. Our desire to care for our bodies should simply be to strengthen them so there is less physical limitation when God says *"Go"* and sends us to do the main thing.

There are two additional snares I would like to address as well, that have the potential of being used by the enemy as a distraction technique.

The Scale
The scale is a tool that gives us information regarding our weight. Yet, we often misuse it to measure our value or worth. If not used wisely, the scale can become a stumbling block of pride. How? If we lose weight, we can get caught up in how great of a job we did and boast of our ability. If we gain weight, we can get caught up in how we keep failing and how we'll never lose weight, which fuels insecurity. One represents high esteem while the other represents low esteem. Both represent pride because both are absorbed with self.

The scale is one of those things that I find requires frequent conversations with God. For some, there is no emotional attachment and it can support a greater understanding and awareness of the body. For others, the scale hinders more than helps and may need to be either reduced or released entirely. I don't have a clear answer for you on the scale because I believe this is an individual conviction. The point is, go to God about it and let Him show you His way for you in it in *every* season. His answer may change, so revisit this often with Him!

The Body Image Trap

Pride is fueled when we focus more on the body image *we* want rather than focusing on the One whose image we are made in. When we can't reach this image, we become discouraged, dissatisfied and discontent. This leaves us so focused on *self* that we miss our God-given purpose and daily call to love God and love others.

Each of us has been uniquely made by God. There is no such thing as a cookie-cutter model. The same way there isn't just one type of flower, tree or bird, there isn't just one physical appearance stencil for all of God's children. If God wanted us all to look the same, weigh the same, and wear the same size, He would have made us that way. But He didn't.

The more we strive to achieve a particular body image, the more distracted we will be from what matters most. We will be so busy giving away our time, money, attention and energy trying to achieve a shape, size or look that we will miss the fullness of contentment found when we keep our focus vertical. Our bodies aren't the focus; Jesus is.

Lastly, I have learned that any version or image of ourselves we try to achieve apart from God will always be lesser. So why do we keep settling for less than God's best? Let's choose to believe that we are fearfully and wonderfully made by God (Psalm 139) and focus more on the One whose image we are made in so we can wholly and humbly reflect His glory.

Pursue Humility

Pursue humility as you show up each day to steward your body. Humility is one key to perseverance. The high esteem of pride leaves you relying on yourself, which becomes too overwhelming, so you give up. The low esteem of pride leaves you insecure and defeated, so you give up. Humility keeps you dependent on God in every way, which helps you persevere.

If our wellness journey is focused only on weight loss, we are opening the door wide for vanity, pride and selfish ambition to enter. Yet, when our focus is on overall health, drawing closer to Jesus, and finding freedom in *Him*, we will remain humbly submissive to His way.

Pride will do whatever it can to save, satisfy, fix and glorify itself. Humility recognizes it's already been saved by grace alone, through Christ alone, and by faith alone. Everything else that follows will be done for His glory alone.

Let's pray for humility. Pursue humility. Practice humility. As you do, continue to rely on the Holy Spirit who is working in you and completing the work God began. Keep your gaze on Christ, your reliance on Christ, and your example Christ. As you stand firm in this battle against pride, know Jesus has already won the war and His grace is sufficient.

PRAYER

Father, help me pursue humility daily in this self-exalting world. Humble service is the path to Kingdom greatness. Reprogram my soul with your Word to remember the world is all about Jesus and not myself. In my battle against pride, keep me from false humility that fails to recognize Your gracious gifts. Instead, help me steward what You have given me as a faithful servant—a servant ready to wear the garment of humility and serve You in whatever way will best build Your Kingdom and praise to Your Name. May my health journey and body only become an extension of my witness and never a hindrance to living purposefully for You. Amen!

REFLECT

❶ Where does pride reign in your life? Ask the Holy Spirit to help you live for God's glory in those areas where you struggle. Ask Him to show you what it looks like to live for the glory of Jesus today.

....
....
....
....
....
....
....

❷ Are you most tempted by the high esteem of pride or low
    esteem?

....
....
....
....
....
....
....
....
....

❸ How can you actively pursue and practice humility in small
    ways today?

....
....
....
....
....
....
....
....
....
....
....
....
....

HONOR YOUR BODY >
ACCEPT YOUR BODY

*A*t first glance, we wouldn't think twice about the phrase "accept your body." I invite you to read with an open mind about how acceptance, while not a wrong first step, is certainly not the extent of our stewardship. First, let's notice the definition differences offered by Oxford Dictionary:[1]

1. *Accepting is a consent to receive something that is offered.*
2. *Honoring is to value, esteem, and regard with great respect.*

To go even one step further when using the word *honor* in relation to the Lord, it's not just normal respect but sacred respect.

With the awareness of the definition differences, we can conclude that to simply accept our bodies is like saying, "God, thank You for this body You gave me. I consent to receive it." In comparison, honoring our bodies would be like saying, "God, thank You for this body You created and gave me to be my 'tent' on earth. In addition to receiving it, I promise to steward it, honor it, and treat it with value as an extension of my reverence for You."

I am also aware that sometimes the struggle isn't going from acceptance to honoring but from hatred to honoring. In this case, I would say that even hating our bodies can be a layer of acceptance. Oftentimes we try even harder to accept our bodies because we've struggled so long with hating them. My prayer is that this chapter prompts deeper and more intimate discussions between you and the Lord to see that He is the remedy for both.

STRONG IN SPIRIT

I first want to expand on the idea of acceptance in relation to our walk with God. It is true that accepting Christ is a beautiful first step in our relationship with Him. For many, however, it has tragically become the only step. Knowing God was never meant to be a one-and-done "I accept" experience. Instead, it's a lifelong journey of desiring Him more and more. We see this kind of desire from Moses (Exodus 13:18–23), David (Psalm 63) and Paul (Philippians 3:8–10).

We've lost the deep intimacy and fellowship of yearning for God, seeking Him, and sacrificing everything so that we may know Him. Knowing God becomes the fuel to knowing Him better, rather than an excuse to settle for knowing Him enough. "I have enough Jesus" is one of the sneakiest lies of the enemy. We can never have enough. There is always more of Him to know, love, seek and crave!

When we come to know the majesty and fullness of God, our worship-filled response will be to honor Him for who He is, what He has done, and with what He gives us—our very life. We cannot honor God if we don't fully know Him. When God reveals Himself to us as our Father, adopting us into His family through faith in Christ, He means for us to have childlike reverence for Him.

Honoring God begins with the renewal of our minds, which then transforms our hearts, altering our responses and actions.

The Renewed Mind

Our desire should be to exalt, honor and magnify Christ with our lives. We cannot do this if we look like the world. In Romans 12:1–2, Paul reveals that the renewal of our minds is the key to transformation. If we want to stop conforming to the patterns of this world and offer our bodies as a living sacrifice, we need to be transformed from the inside out. This ensures that our whole lives become a spiritual act of worship.

Paul says in Ephesians 4:23 to be renewed in the *spirit* of our mind. The mind has a mindset, a viewpoint, and an attitude. This would all be well and good if there wasn't one major problem— our minds are fallen. This means our minds have a spirit and mindset that is blind to the supremacy and holiness of God.

If we want to honor God and revere Him, we must see Him as worthy of such reverence. How do we get there? The Holy Spirit. He is the one who renews our minds and enables us to gaze upon the glory of God (2 Corinthians 3:18).

In one of his sermons, I love how John Piper reveals two directions the Holy Spirit works in our lives: from the outside in and from the inside out. He works from the outside in by exposing our minds to Christ-magnifying truth. The Holy Spirit leads us to read the Bible, understand the Word, hear the gospel, and meditate on who Jesus is. He also works from the inside out by humbling our hard hearts that prevent the seeds of faith from bearing fruit in us, keeping us from seeing God as He truly is.[1]

As the Holy Spirit works in us, we also have work to do. We must be proactive in studying and meditating on God's Word. The Holy Spirit is given not to make our study unneeded or avoidable, but to make it *effective*. We must also be willing to identify the lies that have shaped our lives and what we've been conforming to outside of God's Word. We can't partner with the Holy Spirit in renewal that we don't even know we need.

If you've struggled to see God as holy and worthy of all honor, I encourage you to take the first step of trying to find out why. Then take steps to partner with the Holy Spirit in this renewal process. Pray for and pursue humility. Pursue Christ-magnifying truth. Memorize the truth so it can renew your mind, then speak it out loud! Proverbs 18:21 reminds us that the tongue has the power of life. Therefore, memorize it then declare it out loud, because what you hear often you start to believe. As you do, this will radically change how you come to know God, therefore honoring Him with what He entrusts you with.

The Transformed Heart

Our hearts reveal what we prize, honor and value most. Matthew 6:21 reminds us that where our treasure is, there our hearts will also be. When our minds are renewed by the Holy Spirit and Word of God, our desires shift, and that in turn reframes our affections. The same way the physical heart is the life source of the body, the metaphorical heart represents the life source of our emotions and passions.

We can honor God with our hearts when we surrender our wants, affections and emotions to Him while asking the Holy Spirit to increase our delight in Him.

We can honor God with our hearts when we stop denying or bowing down to our feelings and instead pray them to Him (this is the whole book of Psalms). Not only praying them but then reading the Word and listening for God's answer and Truth to show us His way.

If we are to revere Christ as Lord in our hearts (1 Peter 3:15), then we must value Him more than feelings, success, results and anything else.

A New Response
With renewed minds and transformed hearts, our behaviors not only change, but they look more and more like Jesus. Jesus honored God the Father with His very being, with all He did, and with all He had. He is our example. When our beliefs are aligned with the Word of God and our hearts are captivated by Jesus, our actions follow and represent what the mind believes and the heart receives.

As we grow in our intimate knowledge of who God is, all we do becomes an extension of our worship and is done to honor Him. All we do (this includes the stewardship of our bodies) is now in response to who He is. May our greatest desire and highest priority be to know God more because that is what will impact all we do, why we do it, and how we do it.

With all this in mind, let's get practical with what it means to honor God with our bodies rather than just accepting them.

HEALTHY IN BODY

The same way accepting Christ is the first step but not the only step in our walk with Him, accepting our body is a good place to begin but certainly not the extent of our health journey. I am asking you to open your mind to the possibility that merely accepting your body not only limits how you can honor God with your body but also leaves you with the temptation of complacency or self-sufficiency.

Since we spent so much time on the power of mindset, let's look at the differences in mindset when it comes to honoring versus accepting our bodies.

Honor vs. Accept

"Honor my body" focuses on the Creator, while "accepting my body" focuses on the creation.

Ultimately, honoring our body focuses on the Giver, while accepting it only focuses on the gift itself. The more we fully focus on God, how He made the whole world, created our inmost beings, and bestows honor on us (Psalm 139:13, Psalm 8:4–5), the more our desire increases to honor Him back with all we are, do and have.

How often do you view exercising, eating, drinking, and yes, even sleeping as an act of worship? Maybe the sleeping category feels like a stretch, but even that requires surrender and trusting that God will sustain our work as we honor Him with our rest. The point is, I believe we will honor, care and steward our bodies differently when we view it as an act of worship. However, if we only focus on the acceptance of our bodies, we will be more susceptible to glorifying the one body size trap, being tempted to worship ourselves, striving for success, or defeating driven laziness.

To prevent this, I encourage you to take a moment to remember the Lord—how He sees you, knows you, pursues you and fashions you—every time you're getting ready to work out, eat a meal, or do anything to care for your body. May this prompt you to do all you do with Him, His way, and for His glory.

"Honor my body" is an outside-in and inside-out journey, while "accepting my body" is outside only.

As we've discussed, honoring our bodies requires a heart transformation and the renewal of our minds to see Jesus as our only reward. An inside-out transformation also depends on the power of the Holy Spirit. In contrast, accepting our bodies often relies on our willpower and self-sufficiency, and only manages to change outward behaviors, which are often short-lived.

If you have struggled to honor your body, take time to evaluate if you've been focusing more on behavior change than heart change. You may be doing all the right things (exercising, choosing nutritious foods, etc.) but for all the wrong reasons (pride, envy, attention and selfishness). I invite you to courageously choose the longer journey of partnering with the Holy Spirit to renew your mind and transform your heart. Not only will this change your actions, but the actions you take will be done with one purpose—to honor and worship Christ alone.

> *"Honor my body" comes from a heart content in Christ, while "accepting my body" can come from discontentment and resentment.*

Accepting our bodies can be done with a spirit of resentment. Perhaps we resent not being skinny enough or fit enough. After an exhausting attempt to fix ourselves by ourselves, we settle by simply accepting our insecurities. Unfortunately, this often leads to an absorbed sense of self and bitterness toward our bodies because we aren't at our preferred size or weight. We become so consumed by the bodies we think we *should* have that we miss out on what we *can* do (*through* Christ) with the bodies we *have* been given.

There is a theory out there known as Set Point Theory. *Nourish* by WebMD defines it this way: "Set point theory states that the human body tries to maintain its weight within a preferred range. Many people stay within a more or less small range of body weight throughout their adult life." Now, while I am not sure where I land yet on this theory, I'd like to offer another way to look at it from a Christian point of view: Every person's body has a weight range where it's designed to function and feel best, and that "happy" weight range is different for all. In other words, God picked out a weight range for us all that is perfect for us, that we get to when we are taking care of our bodies, not with extremes or obsession but by listening to the body cues He put in us. It's much harder to feed a spirit of resentment when we are placing our trust in God and His way for us in this.

Contentment protects us from resentment, discontentment, and even entitlement. God's Word says that we can be content and have joy in all circumstances (Philippians 4:11–13, 1 Thessalonians 5:16–18, Philippians 4:4). When we are content in Christ, we no longer strive for a certain body as a way to *finally* feel happy or satisfied. Instead, we honor our bodies from a place of contentment because we are so satisfied with Christ and want to glorify Him in all we do.

Contentment also protects us from the body image trap. While desiring to improve body image is not in and of itself a bad thing, it is one thing that can quickly become an idol in our lives if we aren't daily surrendering it back to God. The struggle of body image is relevant for those with weight to lose and those without weight to lose. You can be at your smallest weight and still struggle with contentment and honoring God with your body. It comes down to your gaze, not your weight. Christ as our gaze is the anchor to a journey of honor and contentment. The moment anything else takes His place, we shift from honoring to obsessing, hating, accepting or resenting.

So how do we grow in contentment? The way of contentment is to be completely captivated by Christ and be fully surrendered to Him. We learn from David in the Psalms how the continual choice to worship and praise God for who He is and His everlasting faithfulness is the key to steady and abiding contentment. In Psalm 23:1 we see David stating how because the Lord was his shepherd, he lacked *nothing*. In Psalm 16:5 he wrote about how the Lord alone was his portion and cup (Psalm 16:5). David didn't hide his honest feelings and thoughts from God, but he always made the effort to shift his focus back to praise, and that made all the difference.

Any time we search for significance, strength or security in anything apart from Him, we have fallen into idolatry. Contentment in Christ means we are so filled with Him that we no longer want the lesser things in this life. The more satisfied we are in Him, the less we will search for the world's version of a full life, because we will already have a *filled* one.

Contentment keeps us secure in Christ so we never lose *joy*, *peace* and *gratitude* in the journey of stewarding our bodies. Contentment helps us distinguish between the eternal and essential needs and the nonessential wants. A godly pursuit of taking care of our bodies with contentment protects the journey from becoming obsessive and self-centered.

I invite you here to identify the things that have been feeding discontentment. Once identified, evaluate with God what may need to be reduced or removed. It might mean taking a month to disconnect from all fitness accounts on social media or taking a break from the scale. While those things can be helpful, if unchecked they can also feed the strive and obsession with your body. This breathing room will allow you to focus on the act of taking care of your body and practice contentment with no "outcome" attachments.

As you reduce or remove, make sure to replace. Replace social media scrolling with more time in prayer and meditating on

God's Word. Replace scale checks with contentment checks. Ask yourself: Did I look for significance, security or strength anywhere outside of Christ today? Did I focus more on what I could do with what I have today through Christ and less on what I did not have? Did I thank God for all I was able to do by His grace today?

In the end, God can do far more with a heart content in Him than with a heart consumed with self. As you let Christ fill you and detach yourself from the things that are "less than," I am confident you will be able to honor your body with Him, His way, and for His glory.

"Honor my body" leads me to be proactive, while "accepting my body" can leave me reactive.

Accepting our bodies has the danger of leaving us passive, mediocre and complacent. We can be quick to accept our bodies with a spirit of defeat and despair because they're not where we want them to be. This can leave us submitting to a life of reactivity with our health (letting life happen rather than intentionally living wisely and well).

For example, when we only accept our body, we don't proactively plan intentional exercise to improve its strength, stamina and mobility. Instead, we live life and leave it to chance whether or not we get some steps in.

In comparison, to honor our body is to be proactive in how we steward it, while consulting God, who made it. When we want to honor something, we go the extra mile and do it with excellence and intentionality. Excellence means showing up, giving our best, and releasing the outcome into His hands. Excellence can still include having high standards, but it removes unrealistic expectations for ourselves.

Honoring our body also requires us to be aware of our body's needs, not just our wants. We cannot sustain the same pace of intensity all the time. When I was in "acceptance mode," I would overlook my body's limits and try to sustain the same intensity no matter what. This left me with a fractured heel, frequent injuries, and complete exhaustion.

When my desire shifted to honoring God with my body, I began taking the time to learn my body's cues for rest, recovery and fuel. God gave us bodies that communicate; we've just been conditioned not to listen to them.

For example, in November 2020, I noticed my body's overall performance was decreasing. I was tired a lot and I wasn't sleeping well. When I stepped back to evaluate my fitness routine for the past year, I noticed it was 80 percent heavy resistance training with components of HIIT (high intensity interval training). This is my favorite style of fitness.

I had a choice to make. I could either push my body to continue doing programs that matched my preferred style, or I could listen and do something that was lower intensity for a few weeks. When I cared more about what would honor my body, I was able to lay down my preference for it. I chose six weeks where I did a barre program, and by January 2021, my body's performance improved significantly. I was sleeping better, and my energy was back.

The same way we cannot honor God until we fully know Him, we cannot honor and steward our bodies well if we are not making the time to understand them. If we constantly see our bodies as problems, we will be in "fix-it" mode rather than "honor" mode.

The more we see our bodies as gifts, the better we can understand them so they can help us live out our purpose with energy, strength, and stamina. What if we take time to write down what we've noticed helps our bodies feel good? What gives them more energy? Leaves them fatigued or sluggish? The more we approach our bodies with kindness, care and grace, the better we will be able to honor them and honor the Lord with them.

Our bodies will either limit or elevate how we live out our purpose to spread the gospel. Therefore, let's make it our aim that our bodies are not neglected or idols. They are simply our "earthly tents" and require proactive care and management.

New Mindset

Knowing this, I would love for you to meditate on a few questions with me. With the new mindset of honoring God with your body and it being an extension of your worship:

1. How differently would you show up for your workout?
2. How differently would you plan and prepare meals?
3. How differently would you schedule rest and recovery for your body?
4. How differently would you extend grace and patience to your body?

I encourage you to pause and really assess if you have been stuck merely accepting the body you've been given or are honoring God with it. Invite the Holy Spirit to renew your mind in how you see the Lord and how you see your body. The more you see with His eyes, the more you will care for what He gives you His way.

PRAYER

Father, You made me and You know me. May my desire today ultimately be to honor You with all I am, all I have, and all I do! Show me how to treat my body like a temple. Teach me to make the right decisions to continually improve my health so that my body is never a barrier to the ministry You call me to on earth. I am ready to release the unhealthy habits and attitudes I have toward my body. Please help me glorify You by nourishing my body well and seeing myself through Your eyes. Forgive me when I believe and act on the lies of the enemy. I'm done magnifying the voice of accusation, forgetting the cross. Help me detach myself from the lesser things and pursue You wholeheartedly. May Your Voice and Your Truth be the loudest in my life. I love You! Amen.

REFLECT

❶ Honoring God begins with the renewal of your mind, which then transforms your heart and alters your response and actions. How can you partner with the Holy Spirit in His inside-out and outside-in work to renew your mind?

....
....
....
....
....
....
....
....
....
....
....

❷ Whether you struggle with accepting or hating your body, how does the view of honoring it change how you care for it?

....
....
....
....
....
....
....
....
....
....
....

❸ How would contentment in Christ change the way you steward your body?

....
....
....
....
....
....
....
....
....
....
....
....
....
....
....

DISCIPLINE > MOTIVATION

"I just need to get motivated."
"I just need to find motivation."
"If only I were more motivated."
"I'm waiting to feel motivated."

How many times have you said to yourself that you're going to start something but end up not following through because you weren't motivated enough? I would then argue that perhaps you were more *interested* than committed. When we are interested in something, we do it when it's convenient and when we *feel* like it. When we are committed to something, we choose discipline and make the necessary sacrifices to see it through. Ultimately, our actions are what reveal whether we are interested or committed.

Most of us squirm at the word *discipline* either because we've turned it into obsession or because we are allergic to effort. To avoid either extreme, let's go to God's Word for the Truth. What we will discover is that motivation is not *all* bad. There is a positive and biblical side to motivation because when its source is correct, it can become a vital source of *fuel* for discipline.

STRONG IN SPIRIT

Christianity is not a mindless experience. Walking with God, choosing His way, and doing all things for Him requires both *His* power and *our* effort. Relying on mere emotions to *feel* like reading the Bible, *feel* like praying, *feel* like obeying, or *feel* like trusting God not only guarantees a mediocre faith but also reflects a heart that is not wholly devoted in its reverence for God.

I have learned that the reason motivation can be unreliable is because it's emotion-driven rather than truth-driven. If we only show up when we feel ready, excited and hopeful, there is a greater chance that we will give up when it gets hard, uncomfortable or discouraging. Emotion-driven motivation fuels inconsistent effort, which only leads to mediocre results. Truth-driven motivation fuels disciplined effort, which leads to consistent progress.

Train in Godliness

Where does our discipline matter most? In 1 Timothy 4:7–8, Paul reminds Timothy to train (or discipline) himself in godliness. Godliness reflects a person who is growing more in the likeness of God and His character. It reflects a person who takes salvation, eternity, and walking with God seriously. When you take something seriously, you train in it.

The aim of Christian discipline, therefore, is to train the body, soul and spirit in the way of godliness. Training requires discipline, perseverance, and an awareness of possible obstacles. We cannot run with perseverance and fix our eyes on Jesus mindlessly (Hebrews 12:1–12). Discipline is necessary.

The Right Motivation

You may be wondering where motivation comes into play. If you have ever found yourself yo-yoing with discipline (been there!), it's very possible that what is missing is the *right* motivation. Motivation is defined as "that which moves one towards an action; that which changes, provokes, or impels our very being."[1]

Paul shows us motivation in action in 1 Corinthians 9:24–27: *"Do you not know that in a race all the runners run, but only one gets the prize? Run in such a way as to get the prize. Everyone who competes in the games goes into strict training. They do it to get a crown that will not last, but we do it to get a crown that will last forever. Therefore I do not run like someone running aimlessly; I do not fight like a boxer beating the air. No, I strike a blow to my body and make it my slave so that after I have preached to others, I myself will not be disqualified for the prize."*

Though we never see the word "motivation" here, doesn't this sound like someone who is motivated? Paul isn't aimlessly running for the discipline of running; he's running with the eternal prize as his aim. The reward Paul is chasing is Christ, and that motivates him to be disciplined, press on, train hard and remain faithful.

I also love the comparison to how athletes train. Athletes live disciplined lives, make endless sacrifices, and willingly choose self-denial because of the particular prize they are pursuing. The prize is their motivation. Paul gets that, which is why he doesn't say, "Don't run to get the prize." Instead, Paul is calling us to run, train, persevere and practice self-discipline because the prize we are chasing is even better because it's not temporary or perishable!

I want to highlight how Paul (and we) still have a responsibility: *to run.* God enabled him to run and persevere, but Paul still had to move his feet. If we are honest with ourselves, sometimes we wish God would just make the path easy, remove temptations, and give us instant success. But if He did, would that teach us to be dependent on Him? Would that build character? Would that move us to practice discipline in an effort to follow through on our commitments? Or would we fall into entitlement, laziness and pride?

God never asks us to do anything apart from His help and power. While the journey won't be effort-free, it will be pressure-free. Why? Because we know that we are not saved by our discipline, effort or performance. We are saved by Christ alone. Therefore, we don't "do" so we can earn. We "do" because of what we've already gained through and in Christ.

Christ Is Our Reward

When our motivation is Christ and He becomes our greatest reward, it changes why and how we do things. When we desire the eternal rewards, the Spirit gives us *more* than the temporary rewards and lesser pleasures this world can offer. We can choose discipline with joy.

If you are struggling to be motivated in your pursuit of Christ, I encourage you to meditate on the gospel message. Without Jesus, we would still be separated from God and on our way to eternal judgment. But God made a way and provided sufficient salvation by His grace for all who believe. Those who believe are then called to go and proclaim the good news of the gospel.

Therefore, Christ Himself, salvation, eternity, and the Great Commission are *more* than sufficient motivators for us to choose discipline. If they are not sufficient motivators, a question we might ask ourselves is, "Where am I struggling with unbelief when it comes to the gospel?" Our mindset influences our motivation. If we believe the Truth, this Truth shapes our minds (thoughts). This then shapes the "why" behind our actions.

To put it plainly, motivation will always let you down if the reward you're chasing is temporary and can only be achieved by your strength. Motivation can support your discipline when Christ is the only reward you're pursuing and His power and *grace* are what you rely on.

Godly Ambition
I feel it necessary to address the words "ambition" and "hustle" here. I am aware they have gotten a bad reputation, thanks to living in a culture that overworks, never rests, and pursues selfish ambition and its own glory. However, I believe that as Christians we are to be the *most* ambitious. The difference is our ambition and our hustle are Kingdom-driven. They are *motivated* by Christ, *powered* by Christ, and *for* the glory of Christ.

When I read about Paul's life in the New Testament, all I can say is...brother was ambitious! He boldly hustled for the Kingdom of God. He didn't burn out because he relied on God's power and direction. He didn't lose motivation because the reward he pursued could never lose its value. He didn't get discouraged by his weakness because he learned that God's grace is sufficient (2 Corinthians 12:9). He didn't get lost in the selfish side of ambition because he actively pursued humility and only gave God glory.

Looking at Paul's life, I used to think to myself, "Well, that's because he's Paul. He was special." I will never forget this quote by John Eldredge in his book *Walking With God* that changed how I read God's Word: "The Bible isn't a book of exceptions; it's a book of examples."[2]

Really let this sink in. Paul wasn't special; he was simply completely devoted to Christ. The same Holy Spirit who worked in and through Paul is in you and me. The same Holy Spirit that covered Paul's weakness with God's grace is in you and me. The same Holy Spirit that empowered Paul to run the race with discipline and perseverance is in you and me.

When to Be Cautious With Discipline

I have three warnings when it comes to discipline. First, it's really easy for discipline to become legalistic if we lose sight of God's grace, His leading, and our wrong motives. Discipline is not opposed to grace; it's *powered* by grace. Discipline requires your effort, and grace reminds you of God's power. Don't fall into the trap of extremes of striving or laziness.

Second, be cautious that your discipline isn't too rigid, otherwise you won't want to show up. If your quiet-time structure with the Lord is too rigid, you won't delight in showing up. If your workout routine is too rigid, you won't delight in showing up. If your nutrition plan is too rigid, you won't delight in showing up. Get my point? Discipline is meant to create consistent rhythms in your life that bring peace and fuel purpose. I encourage you to seek the Lord for His definition of a consistent and fruitful rhythm for this season of your life, a rhythm that invites discipline in a way that doesn't overwhelm or suffocate you. There may absolutely be times when it's appropriate to change or tweak the rhythm. I remember when I would have specific rhythms around my exercise, nutrition, and even my office hours! Although these rhythms were set and overall beneficial, there were unique moments where they actually hindered more than helped. In this case, I would pray and ask God for His wisdom in tweaking them.

Lastly, we never want to be *so* disciplined that we miss God's direction. There have been times when I've been so disciplined in my Bible reading that I struggle to go "off-plan" when God is leading me a different way in my quiet time. The same can be with our health. We can be so disciplined with exercise that we miss our body's cues for extra rest days or lower intensity days. Discipline is meant to be a catalyst to freedom, not another form of slavery.

How can discipline be freedom? For example, when we've built the discipline of studying the Word, we can deviate from our Bible-reading plan and follow the Holy Spirit's prompting without being susceptible to neglecting time in the Word altogether. Discipline also becomes freedom when our ultimate desire is to love and please the Lord. John Piper said it best: "When you are transformed in Christ, you love to do what you ought to do. That's freedom."[3]

Discipline Is a Choice
Discipline is not something we have but something we must choose.

- Choosing discipline means no longer bowing down to emotions.
- Choosing discipline is choosing truth-driven purpose over emotion-driven preference.
- Choosing discipline is choosing commitment over interest.
- Choosing discipline is choosing self-control.
- Choosing discipline is choosing what we want *most* instead of what we want *now* (props to Abraham Lincoln[4] for that one!).
- Choosing discipline is choosing what will matter in *eternity* over the things that are *temporary*.

The more we view God as holy and desire Him above all else, the more we will love to be disciplined in the things we ought to be disciplined in. Discipline doesn't have to be all grit and duty. With time, it can be chosen with joy and delight! I remember hearing that it takes doing something twenty-one times before it stops feeling uncomfortable. Twenty-one times! Don't give up. Lean in and trust that the Holy Spirit can turn what starts as discipline into desire. Declare Galatians 6:9 with me: *"Let us not become weary in doing good, for at the proper time we will reap a harvest if we do not give up."*

HEALTHY IN BODY

The "Quick Fix" Appeal

Many wellness companies offer shortcuts and quick fixes because they know that anytime something takes real effort, time and discipline, people lose motivation. We don't want to give up our preferences, conveniences, control or comfort. The less perseverance is required, the more interested we are. The easier and lazier an option is, the more people will get in line.

If our greatest desire is for our character to be refined and made more like Christ through our health, why are we chasing solutions that require no character growth? I will be the first to admit that there was a time I only chased the quick fix. If it meant I had to deny my desires or cravings, I didn't want it. My mindset was, "I don't want to change any of my poor habits, but I want results as though I did." Yikes. God got ahold of my heart and showed me how pursuing discipline in my health was another way I could honor Him. Not only so, but with each act of discipline, I was relying on the Holy Spirit to help me practice self-control and actively die to my flesh. I love how my friend Somer Phoebus puts it: "Self-control is not a mindset or a lifestyle; it's a funeral for your flesh."[5]

When our motivation is to honor God with our bodies, prevent our bodies from being a barrier to anything He asks us to do, and use our bodies to strengthen and serve others, it changes how and why we steward our health. When our "why" is purpose-driven, we won't be seduced by shortcuts or susceptible to quitting when things get hard.

The Disconnect Between Knowledge and Action

"I know what I need to do; I just struggle to do it." I've heard this often as a wellness coach, and I too have struggled to put knowledge to action. We know that to have healthy bodies we need to exercise consistently, nourish well, sleep well, hydrate well, etc., but we lack the discipline to do it. Sometimes what we need is a dose of truth, and sometimes what we need is a dose of grace. I am not sure what season you're in with this, so I will speak to both.

To my friend who is in need of grace, you may know what to do, but due to overwhelm, you feel paralyzed in taking any steps. If this is you, I'd like to remind you of three things:

1. First, Jesus invites you to come and cast your cares on Him, because He cares for you (1 Peter 5:7). Sometimes we need to lose the weight emotionally, mentally, and even spiritually before we can pursue discipline in the physical. Is there something you need to cast in the direction of Christ? Is there something you need to bring before the Lord to discern if it needs to be reduced, released or renewed? Sometimes this is where we need to begin.

2. Second, revisit the habits you're pursuing for your health and make sure they are realistic and sustainable. Maybe instead of doing thirty- to forty-minute workout programs, you start with one that is ten minutes. Or maybe instead of trying to prep all your meals, you only prep breakfasts. Small steps are still significant steps.

3. Third, we focus a lot on habit replacement, but sometimes it's easier to start with habit addition. If the idea of replacing a lot of habits is daunting, try adding one new healthy habit. Yes, even if it means nothing else changes, that's fine. Just add one healthy habit you can sustain

and be consistent with. Maybe it's more water or natural activity instead of a structured workout. Once you've got it, add another. With time, the unhealthy habits reduce because the healthy ones increase.

If you're my friend who knows what to do but simply won't do it, are you open to some truth in love? If so, I'd like to share two Scriptures with you.

To learn, you must love discipline; it is stupid to hate correction.
—Proverbs 12:1 (ESV)

Knowing what to do isn't enough. Sam Manuel put it well: "Knowledge without application and discipline will not produce transformation."[6] We must act on what we know. This is just as relevant when it comes to taking care of our bodies. What is one step you can take today in caring for your body based on a simple truth you know? For example, if you know that nighttime snacking is a struggle, first acknowledge if it's real hunger or a habit. Then, one step can be to brush your teeth earlier or opt for tea.

Sluggards do not plow in season; so at harvest time they look but find nothing.
—Proverbs 20:4

I really want to unpack this verse thoroughly because it was what stopped me dead in my "entitlement track" back when I first had the desire to get healthy. What we see is that when we are disciplined in plowing, we can expect a harvest. If we are too lazy to plow, we shouldn't expect a harvest. If we want to reap, we must sow. In this case, we are identifying plowing and sowing as proactively taking care of our bodies. Sowing puts knowledge to action and requires discipline and effort.

One of the first questions I had when I was first introduced to this verse was, "Why are the sluggards even looking at harvest time if they know they have not been plowing?" Then I realized that there may have been a spirit of entitlement. I am sure they had an awareness of when the seasons were and an abundance of knowledge about plowing. Perhaps they thought they might reap something while doing nothing because somehow it was unfair if they didn't?

When we don't act on what we know is true (small steps count!), a spirit of entitlement can grow. Have you ever felt frustrated when you aren't seeing certain results? Has that frustration ever stemmed from the mindset of "I know all these things about health, so why am I not seeing results?"

You're not alone. If you didn't know, I am a closet nerd (only about certain things). I love to research things and grow my knowledge on what I value. With health, there was a point in my life where I would spend *hours* researching how to take care of my body and *zero* hours putting into action what I learned. I would get so resentful and angry because I knew so much and could even give people solid health advice, but for some reason I wasn't seeing changes in my own health! Cue Proverbs 20:4. Ouch. I learned then that, while knowledge can be valuable, without action it's powerless.

I also learned that "research" can be overdone and cause paralysis from action. Since then, I have personally learned to pause on what I am learning. If I have something I can apply that is realistic and sustainable, I focus on applying the knowledge with discipline before going back to learn more. This has kept me from overwhelm, idleness, entitlement and passivity!

I am encouraging you to take a moment to self-reflect with me. Is it possible that the reason there has been no change is because there has been no consistent action, sacrifice or discipline? This isn't about trying your way harder. It's about asking God to show you His way. As He does, surrender, put in the effort, then surrender again. His power is accessible in the everyday mundane (including what you eat and drink). Small, truth-driven choices, with consistency, time and discipline, can bring about big change!

The 5 Ps to Pursue with Discipline

No matter where you are in your journey, I'd like to share with you the five "P"s to pursue discipline that have really helped me care for my body intentionally.

Pray
1 Chronicles 16:11 and Matthew 6:33 remind us to seek God *first*, not as a last resort but as our very first step. Prayer is one way for us to align ourselves with God and His purpose so that in communication with Him, we learn His way for us.

Before setting goals of discipline in your health, be honest with the Lord about where you are. Ask Him to show you how He can be the point of it all. As you do, ask Him for strength to help keep your eyes focused on Him and for discipline when things get hard.

Prioritize

As you get ready to pursue the activities required to take care of your body, recognize that discipline requires sacrifice and surrender. We have to be willing to sacrifice the things that are less important for those more important. Until you see taking care of your body as a valuable priority, you won't prioritize it. For example, prioritizing a morning routine that includes time for Bible study and exercise might mean sacrificing screen time so you can get to bed earlier. Another example might be how prioritizing nourishing your body with greater intention might mean reducing how often you eat out.

Prepare

No more "winging it." When we plan and prepare for something, it shows that we are serious about it. For example, if you want to nourish your body better and more purposefully, spend thirty minutes every weekend planning your dinners for the week. One tip would be to start small by picking one meal to prepare for each day, then work your way up to more if you want to, so you take the guesswork out of it. Discipline is difficult to build when the road to get there is an afterthought. Redeem the energy, time and resources God has given you to prepare for what you want to be disciplined in.

Pursue

Discipline is action. It's time to execute what you know, prayed for, prioritized and prepared for. Colossians 3:23 reminds us that no matter what we do, we are to work at it with all our hearts for the Lord! Focus on taking one small step at a time, remembering that discipline is a muscle that takes training and action, just like physical muscles.

I also highly recommend accountability here. Share your priorities with someone you trust, and ask them to hold you accountable! An important element of training and discipline is allowing wise counsel to teach, challenge, encourage, and call you up according to the Truth.

Patience
It's okay to grow slow. Be careful of saying, "I am not seeing results fast enough or big enough." Fast enough compared to who? The faster we get rid of toxic comparison, the more we can patiently endure in the race we are running. Remember, God Himself is patient and does not rush. Why do we rush, then? Rushed results rarely stick. When we choose the longer way paved by discipline, we can establish healthy and holy habits that are steadfast.

Can I talk about the scale here? For those that use the scale, be patient with the scale. I address the scale in several other chapters, but here I feel it necessary to remind you that if you are on a weight loss journey with the Lord, oftentimes the numbers have to be shaky before they are solid. If, as you lose weight, you hit a milestone weight and then the next day are up a little again, don't fret. That number will be a little shaky at first before it's solid and you can work on the next goal. The good news is that when we are patient, seek the Lord, and keep learning in the shaking, what remains will be unshakable.

Finally, patience also must be extended toward yourself and your weaknesses. Focus more on God's mercies being new every morning. As I said before, discipline is not opposed to grace, so rely on His grace! We can be quick to criticize ourselves when we make a mistake or go "off-plan." The next thing we know, we are "off the wagon." I may get a little sassy here, but I want to be perfectly clear: there is no wagon. Diet culture has convinced us that if we are not on a diet wagon, we are not taking care of our bodies. I am here to tell you this is nonsense.

A wagon, to me, is something I hop on when I *feel* like it and then hop off when I don't. A "wagon" mindset relies on motivation *only*. We can then make the argument that discipline can't grow in a "wagon" mindset. Discipline requires commitment to one race in one direction. It's one race. Just because you stumble, struggle or fail doesn't mean you left the race, because the race is not a wagon.

It would be much easier to convince ourselves that God doesn't want us to be disciplined in our wellness so we can do things our way. Discipline and self-control aren't a suggestion, however; they're a command that involves every area of our life. When we ultimately love God more than ourselves, we love the discipline that leads us closer to Him. When we rely on God for growth in discipline more than ourselves, we succeed more and fail less. The right motivation, purpose and grace all help fuel discipline.

PRAYER

Father, thank You for giving me a spirit of power, love and self-discipline. I surrender to Your will and Your way for my life. Lord, I struggle when it comes to doing what I need to do. I don't want my feelings to control me. Forgive me when I bow down to my emotions rather than Your Word and Your Truth. Help me to develop discipline in all areas of my life, including my health. Your Word says that through You, I can do anything. I believe that and receive it today! Thank You for the daily opportunity I have to steward the body You gave me. Give me wisdom to know when to push with joy and when to pull back with peace. Help me to make choices today that are beneficial for my body and that help, not hinder. Keep me in step with You. Amen.

REFLECT

❶ How does Christ being your reward and motivation change your journey of discipline?

....

....

....

....

....

....

....

❷ "Discipline is in between goals and results." What areas of your life have not been growing or are becoming stagnant due to lack of discipline?

....
....
....
....
....
....
....
....
....
....
....
....
....

❸ What are some rhythms you can establish today with God that enable you to steward well what He has given you?

....
....
....
....
....
....
....
....
....
....
....
....
....

HOLINESS > FREEDOM

*T*he first time I heard this concept of holiness being greater than freedom was in Lisa Whittle's book *Jesus Over Everything*. I found it so convicting and true, and wanted to unpack it with you in relation to our wellness.

We see how in Christ we are free in Scriptures like Galatians 5:13, 2 Corinthians 3:17, John 8:32, 1 Peter 2:16–17, Romans 6:18, Romans 8:2, Romans 6:22 and Psalm 119:45. We also cannot forget that because God is holy, and we are called to be holy, we now have a new *purpose* for our freedom—His purpose—and that is to glorify Him, become more like Him, and make Him known.

I'm not going to sugarcoat it; this chapter was daunting to write. To try to capture the holiness of God and our journey to be holy as He is holy through words on a page did not seem sufficient. I want you to know that because of this, right now in this moment, I am praying for us that the Lord will open our eyes, soften our hearts, and renew our minds to see Him in His fullness. I am asking the Holy Spirit to do what only He can do and reveal God's glory to us.

STRONG IN SPIRIT

Let's begin our time together here with a question (bonus points if you take out your journal or a piece of paper to process this): Do you truly revere and see God as holy? Do you view Him as your equal? Why or why not?

I have learned from personal experience that the moment we stop seeing God as holy and sanctified (set apart), it becomes easier for us to misuse and abuse our freedom. Yet, when we truly see, revere and understand Him as holy, we submit every area of our life under Him, place Him over everything, and use our freedom for righteousness.

There are many Scriptures that address the topic of holiness (1 Thessalonians 4:7, Romans 12:1, Romans 6:22, 2 Timothy 1:9, 1 Thessalonians 5:23, 2 Timothy 2:21). For now, I want to share with you 1 Peter 1:13–16 (Amplified Bible):

So prepare your minds for action, be completely sober [in spirit— steadfast, self-disciplined, spiritually and morally alert], fix your hope completely on the grace [of God] that is coming to you when Jesus Christ is revealed. [Live] as obedient children [of God]; do not be conformed to the evil desires which governed you in your ignorance [before you knew the requirements and transforming power of the good news regarding salvation]. But like the Holy One who called you, be holy yourselves in all your conduct [be set apart from the world by your godly character and moral courage]; because it is written, "You shall be holy (set apart), for I am holy."

I encourage you to read the first twelve verses for the full context. Peter is addressing the topic of new birth in Christ and explaining how we can rejoice in tribulation. Ultimately, if we want to rejoice in suffering, we must prepare our minds for action. We cannot prepare passively!

This kind of preparation requires full focus on the Lord and His holiness while putting an end to distraction and division in our hearts and minds. It means no longer giving God just a piece of our heart or only pursuing Him with a small corner of our mind. It means we no longer see our faith as a hobby and God as our "buddy." Instead, there is an active and passionate pursuit for holiness because He is holy. After all, God commands it, which tells us that not only is it possible, it's nonnegotiable.

I find where we sometimes get stuck in our journey to be holy as He is holy is that we try to muscle our way to holiness. It's as though we are on this spiritual balance beam striving to be like Jesus, but constantly losing our footing and falling off. Just when we start conquering sin in one area, another area pops up. Then the journey of holiness starts to seem daunting, defeating, and perhaps at times even hopeless.

While God's heart is that we absolutely do become holy as He is holy, He also knows that holiness cannot be achieved by our efforts. Holiness comes about through a genuine relationship with God alone, and it's His Spirit that does the work in us. My hope is that as we unpack the nature of God and our response to Him, we never forget that holiness increases in our lives as we seek the Lord and experience the fullness of His holiness, love, forgiveness, grace and nearness to us.

God is Holy

God is set apart and wholly separate from sin. He is perfect. He lacks nothing. God's holiness isn't just a part of who He is; it *is* who He is. It's His essence. Everything He does, and everything He is, is holy. God is holy in *every* attribute and action; He is holy in justice, love, mercy, wisdom, power, patience, anger, grace, faithfulness, compassion, justice and sovereignty. This should leave us in complete peace, awe and surrender.

If we believe He is holy (infinitely beyond us) and all He does is holy, then we can read Isaiah 55:8–9 with new eyes: *"For my thoughts are not your thoughts, neither are your ways my ways,"* declares the Lord. *"As the heavens are higher than the earth, so are my ways higher than your ways and my thoughts than your thoughts."*

We will be able to resist complaining when we don't like God's way when we believe His way is holy. We will stop worrying because we trust His wisdom to be holy. We will stop comparing His way to our way when we finally cut Him off from all our human scales and measurements. When we see God's absolute perfection, we will realize He could never sin against us. This alone deepens our trust in Him!

We Must Be Holy as He Is Holy

What does God's holiness have to do with us? Well, *everything*! We cannot live the life God intended for us to live apart from walking in righteousness. To walk in righteousness, we need God's love and presence to shine light on our sin and brokenness, so that we may confess, repent and experience a life of holiness and freedom as His children.

In 1 Peter 1:13–16 we see that because holiness is the essence of God's character, it becomes our calling as His children by inheritance. Paul Tripp explains it well: "If you are God's child, you stand before him as righteous because the perfect righteousness of Jesus has been given over to your personal account. But there's a second aspect of this—you are holy because you have been bought with the blood of Jesus and you are not your own (see 1 Corinthians 6:19, 20)."[1]

It's through the blood of Jesus that God is now able to flood the earth with His presence! Really allow that to sink in. Christ defeated the power of sin and death and made the way for you and me to be the new temples of God's holy and powerful presence. With this in mind, are we experiencing the fullness of what has been made available to us through Christ? Are we living out of the holiness of the very Spirit who dwells within us and has made us righteous new creations (2 Corinthians 5:17, 2 Corinthians 5:21)?

As we come to see the reality of God's presence in our lives, we can begin to realign our lives with the will of the Spirit. It's as we spend time encountering the holiness of God that we will be transformed from the inside out. We were made in the image of God to be imitators of God. We have been set apart by God's grace for His purpose. This means our allegiance is no longer to our own kingdom or to build our name, but to the progress of *His* Kingdom and to build *His* Name. The same way He is set apart, we are called to be set apart.

Have you ever noticed in the Old Testament how lifeless objects are deemed as holy? Things like tithes, linen, pots, silver, etc.? Anything put at God's disposal and for His exclusive use is holy because it is wholly devoted to Him and separated unto Him.

We are the same. The depth of our devotion to Christ affects the degree of our holiness. To be holy means that there is no area in our life that isn't submitted to Him. All we are and all we have belongs to Him and is set apart for His holy and exclusive purpose.

A final point here: In addition to holiness being marked by our devotion to Him, I believe it's also tied to our contentment in Him. When we are content in Christ, we do not seek any other form of pleasure or devote ourselves to anything else but Him. Are your loyalty and devotion divided? This is often an indication of a heart not yet fully content in Christ.

His Power and Our Efforts

Now, none of us can be perfectly holy on this side of heaven, but this *is* to be our aim! God would not call us to be holy if it were impossible for us to be. By His grace, He makes us able. He is our perfecter (Hebrews 12:2). We aren't called to strive for perfection but to surrender to the One who perfects us day by day. We see God's power and our efforts come together once again in these two passages:

> *Now may the God of peace himself sanctify you completely, and may your whole spirit and soul and body be kept blameless at the coming of our Lord Jesus Christ.*
> —1 Thessalonians 5:23

> *Therefore, if anyone cleanses himself from what is dishonorable, he will be a vessel for honorable use, set apart as holy, useful to the master of the house, ready for every good work.*
> —2 Timothy 2:21

The Holy Spirit's mission in our hearts is to sanctify us, and we must be diligent in cleansing ourselves from what is dishonorable. This is where our freedoms come into play and require a "holiness check."

Use Freedom Wisely

When we fix our hopes on the holy grace of God and we revere Him as holy, we don't want to use our freedom to please our flesh but to be set apart for His holy purpose.

> *For you were called to freedom, brothers. Only do not use your freedom as an opportunity for the flesh, but through love serve one another.*
>
> —Galatians 5:13 (ESV)

> *Live as people who are free, not using your freedom as a cover-up for evil, but living as servants of God.*
>
> —1 Peter 2:16–17 (ESV)

> *But now that you have been set free from sin and have become slaves of God, the fruit you get leads to sanctification and its end, eternal life.*
>
> —Romans 6:22 (ESV)

What we see right away from these verses is that there is a responsibility that comes with freedom. We are to use our freedom to deny ourselves, living according to God's holy Word and holy way. This denial is not meant to be a resentful and obligatory decision but a joy-filled one. How? When we meditate on Jesus's love and sacrifice on the cross and we see how wholly devoted He is to us, we will want to become as wholly devoted to Him and use our freedom for Him.

Jesus's Example

In John 17:9, Jesus is praying to the Father on our behalf, saying, "For them I sanctify myself, that they too may be truly sanctified." For our sake, Jesus totally devoted Himself to our salvation. This makes me want to leap off my chair and fall to my knees in complete awe, gratitude and praise.

In Philippians 2:1–11, we see Jesus, who is fully God and fully man, not consider equality with God something to be used to His own advantage. Instead, He uses His infinite freedom to become a servant and put our interests above his own earthly comforts. Even more so, He freely gives up His life for us.

This should move us to confidently say, "Holy Spirit, I lay my will down that I may be wholly devoted to God's purpose. Instead of doing what I want, I change my wants and use my freedom to be a servant to love God and others."

Freedom His Way

While worldly freedom says, "I can do what I want, when I want, and how I want," godly freedom says, "Because I am so free and satisfied in Christ, I joyfully release earthly freedoms that hinder holiness." When we see God's holiness and are ruled by Christ, we no longer resist a life of submission or conviction. Instead, we embrace it, appreciate it, and see boundaries as freedom, not limitations.

Now the question is, are we using our freedom to make much of Christ, become more like Christ, and love others? Or are we using our freedom for our gain? We are ultimately set free from sin to become slaves to righteousness. Though I've mentioned this quote in the previous chapter, it's worth mentioning again: "When you are transformed in Christ, you love to do what you ought to do. That's freedom."

Start asking yourself if the freedoms you are choosing are aiding in holiness or complicating and compromising it. This isn't about legalism with a list of dos and don'ts. It *is* about receiving conviction from a holy God with peace because we know that some things, though permissible, are not beneficial (1 Corinthians 6:12).

The moment we stop revering God as holy and love the world and freedom more than Jesus, the more vulnerable we are to temptation and sin. Everything in this world will fade away. Everything people crave will fade away. Really let this sink in! Wouldn't you, then, want to redeem your time doing what will please God and have lasting fruit in eternity?

I love how Lisa Whittle says, "Denial of freedom, in cases where flesh would win over spirit, is caring enough about the soul and about Jesus that we deny things that won't benefit our relationship with Him even though our freedom may allow for them." With that, what are the freedoms hindering your holiness, that aren't making you more like Jesus, or that are leaving you wasting valuable and limited time here? It takes several serious heart checks to identify them, and it's uncomfortable. We must be devoted to prayer, the studying of God's Word, and a life of self-denial to choose the holy path. This is ultimately His way, and it's supplied by His power.

HEALTHY IN BODY

While there are many things in Scripture that are clearly stated as righteous or sinful, other things aren't as clear and require personal conviction and conversation with God. This is why I am not going to clearly say "do this" or "don't do that" in this section.

Instead, I am inviting you to search your soul and be honest with yourself. Where have you abused freedoms when it comes to working out or nutrition? Where have your preferences and wants come at the cost of trusting God, depending on God, and being content in Him alone? What are the areas that require more self-control instead of self-consumption?

Personal Convictions

I have shared with you my past addiction with food and exercise. During that season, God convicted me to take an extended fast from exercise (food had its own journey). I remember feeling so conflicted by His prompt. "But exercise is good for my body!" "But it gives me energy!" "But I am free to do it!" But, but, but.

Was God really asking me to give up a good thing? Yes, He was, because it was turning into a god. Exercise was becoming my master. If I didn't burn "X" amount of calories, I would be frustrated. If I didn't sweat, I did a second workout. If I had to take a rest day because my body was completely burnt out, I would overeat and sulk. This wasn't freedom; this was bondage.

I am so thankful God doesn't leave us to ourselves. Removing exercise for a period of time created a sacred space where I could surrender my control, fears and pride. The whole point of fasting is to intensify our gaze on the One we really need and remember that He is the only source of pleasure we are to pursue. During this fast, my eyes were opened to His holiness. I could finally see how I had turned something beneficial for my body into something destructive. This marked the beginning of learning how to do things with Him, His way, and for His glory.

Another example was around the topic of modesty. Running my own faith-based wellness business meant taking progress pictures regularly to show proof that our programs and resources work. However, my pride started to increase, and I was no longer sharing my photos with the right heart posture. It was a humility issue. God convicted me in 2017 and prompted me to eliminate all skin-revealing progress photos. Though I was *free* to keep sharing, the cost would be lack of holiness and, ultimately, disobedience toward God. Not worth it! After confessing and repenting, I willingly gave up this specific freedom because I trusted God. I trusted His holy wisdom. I trusted His way for me. I began to see how much easier it was to discern which freedoms fueled or interrupted my abiding in Christ when I was truly content in Him and pursuing holiness.

Have To vs. Want To

A heart that is oriented to the holiness of God and pursues holiness doesn't see denial of certain freedoms or pleasing God as a "have to" but as a "want to." It becomes the delight of our hearts to live His way and for His glory! I love how Ray Stedman puts it: "True Christianity is to manifest genuinely Christ-like behavior by dependence on the working of the Spirit of God within, motivated by a love for the glory and honor of God."[3]

I invite you to consider these questions: What freedoms in your health are no longer honoring God, inviting peace, benefiting your body, or allowing you to serve well? What freedoms are helping your body but hurting your soul? What freedoms have made holiness an afterthought? Is there anything that, while permissible, is not currently beneficial?

The more we know God, believe Him and trust Him, the more willing we will be to add, release or reduce whatever He individually calls us to. The most important thing is to ensure He is the one doing the leading.

For example, if you want to cut out something from your diet for a period of time, make sure it's coming from a place of conviction, not restriction. If it's God convicting you, He will enable and empower you to do it. If it's driven by restriction, ask yourself why. What is the motive? To draw closer to the Lord or as a shortcut to progress?

When we release things from a place of restriction, we rely on our willpower, which doesn't get us far. Not only so, but because there is no real inner healing, the struggle will come back with a vengeance. When it's led by God, it will be powered by God. While it will still require effort, discipline and sacrifice, the process will be filled with His peace. If it's led by you, pressure will build and the chains will only get heavier.

Love and Free Will

It is normal to wonder why God would give us free will and then advise us to use our free will His way. The answer is love. He is love, and His way is love. God gives us freedom so we can hopefully choose love. Love, in its most basic definition, is the will to do good.

For example, let's say you are the owner of a car. With your free will, you can choose what to use as gas for your car. You could use water, juice, gasoline, chlorine, etc. If you care for your car, you will choose gas because it's what helps your car perform best.

Our bodies are the same. When we love our bodies, we have the will to do good toward them. We fuel them with what is best, beneficial, and enhances their performance. It's not about loving our bodies because of the way they look but because of who our Creator is and what our bodies enable us to do.

> *Therefore, I urge you, brothers and sisters, in view of God's mercy, to offer your bodies as a living sacrifice, holy and pleasing to God—this is your true and proper worship.*
> —Romans 12:1

Although this verse in Romans 12 is likely familiar to you, I invite you to read it a few times slowly. Here is what we see (and what it has to do with pursuing holiness).

- *Therefore*: Paul's statement about offering our bodies as a living sacrifice is based on all he initially shared about who God is and what God has done in Romans 11 (which I encourage you to go read!)
- *In view of God's mercy*: Here we see that offering our bodies as living sacrifices is not something we are asked to do on our own strength. Instead, it is because of God's mercy and by His mercy. It's God's mercy that helps us to offer our everyday lives and surrender them to Him as an offering.

- *Offer*: Paul is making it clear that this offering is a choice. It is not forced. We are to offer our very beings by choice unto the Lord.
- *Your bodies*: This means our whole selves. Our spirits, minds, bodies and souls. God wants our whole selves, not just our performances or efforts. He doesn't just want our works but for us to give Him our whole hearts.
- *As a living sacrifice*: Think about it with me. Would you consider your body a good master? I would argue that it's not. The body is a great servant, but making it our master leads us down a path of a flesh-led life rather than Spirit-led. By offering them as living sacrifices, we keep our bodies in their proper place, submitted to God.
- *Holy and pleasing to God*: As we offer our bodies as living sacrifices, God burns away any impurities and makes us holy. He shakes things up so what remains is solid, unshakable, and built upon Him.

I pray this gives you a new perspective and understanding of Romans 12:1. Because of God's mercy and by His mercy (with God), we get to offer our bodies as living sacrifices to keep them in their proper place and prevent sin. As we do this, it is God who makes us holy!

Lean In

His Holy Spirit is in you! The question is, are you listening? Are you asking? Are you willing? His mission is to sanctify us, and this should give us overwhelming peace and assurance. While getting healthy requires our effort, holiness requires God. As long as we are humbling ourselves daily to His leading, revering Him as holy, and desiring to be holy as He is holy, we won't stray too far when we miss the mark. We can rest in His forgiveness and allow it to be the foundation on which we live in the freedom bought for us by the blood of Jesus.

PRAYER

Father, You are holy and deserve all the glory and praise! I desire to be holy and set apart for Your purpose. I desire to live my life in a manner that is worthy of You and pleasing to You. Please search my heart and show me where I am not revering You as holy and living for my gain. Purify my heart, cleanse my thoughts, and examine the motives behind my attitudes and actions. Please guide me into a process of holiness that is marked by Your grace, love and nearness. If something in my life dishonors You, I don't want it! No matter how painful it may be to remove or reduce, I love You more. Help me to use the freedom You give me for Your glory and the good of others. I love you. Amen.

REFLECT

❶ Allow the holiness and love of God to reveal any unconfessed sins or freedoms you've grown to love more than God Himself.

....
....
....
....
....
....
....
....
....
....
....

❷ What freedoms in your health are no longer honoring God, benefiting your body, or allowing you to serve well?

....
....
....
....
....
....
....
....
....
....
....

❸ How have you noticed decisions being made from a mindset of restriction rather than the heart posture of conviction?

....
....
....
....
....
....
....
....
....
....
....
....
....
....

14

BELIEFS > BEHAVIOR

*F*air warning, this is the chapter where my former licensed therapist comes out! It's a subject I get extremely passionate about because it's not talked about enough. Our mental, physical and spiritual health are all connected, and our beliefs shape all three. Our behaviors and actions are ultimately a representation of our core (strongest) beliefs.

So often, we focus on behavior modification apart from belief identification and transformation. Have you ever stopped to really identify what you believe about God? Yourself? Your neighbor? The world? We can't use God's Word to effectively counter something we either don't believe in or know exists. A courageous introspection of our beliefs is necessary!

Our core beliefs shape our desire and commitment to live healthy and holy lives. If our beliefs do not align with God's Word, we are always vulnerable to pride, broken relationships (including our relationship with our own bodies), and attacks from the enemy. I will share examples of exactly that with you in the Healthy in Body section. I will tell you eight things I wish I believed about my body that could have saved me a lot of heartache.

Friends, we will struggle to be effective for God's Kingdom if we are enslaved to old thinking, false beliefs and shame. It's time our beliefs are based on Truth and not our emotions, assumptions or circumstances. It's time we stop trying new behaviors without changing old beliefs. Amen?

STRONG IN SPIRIT

Have you ever found yourself brushing past certain parts of the Bible? Have you ever stopped to actually ask *why*? I have had to address this within myself and have discovered that it is either because it drags on (cue Leviticus; I am working on it) or because something is contradicting my core beliefs. I know, I know. It took me a while to admit I might have core beliefs that are *not* aligned with God's Word. But the sooner I was able to admit it, the sooner the renewal of my mind could begin. The same is true for you! Just like a doctor can't heal what isn't first revealed, we cannot use God's Word to renew our minds or counter false beliefs without first identifying our misaligned beliefs.

Let's say, for example, that due to painful life circumstances or something someone once said, you now have a core belief that you are unloved, unknown and unwanted. Because you believe this, you will subconsciously resist parts of the Bible that tell you that you are loved (Romans 8:35–39, John 3:16), you are known (Psalm 139:1–6, John 10:14), and you are wanted (John 3:16, Revelation 21:3–4, Matthew 11:28–30).

Does this sound familiar? If so, you're not alone! The good news is Jesus is near. He is willing and able to heal every wound and tear down every false belief with Truth because He is the Truth. Our first step is to sit long enough in the uncomfortable process of identifying and revealing our own beliefs, so that we can humbly repent, be uplifted by His grace and love, and replace the lies with His Truth.

What I have learned about beliefs is that they are controlled either by our old natures or our new natures. To begin the process of renewing our beliefs, we must let God renew our minds, pursue a Kingdom mindset, and abide in God's Truth as our new filter.

Let God Renew Your Mind

Your mind is where the enemy will attack most because it's the battlefield where the war for your purpose, identity, emotions and impact is won or lost. Your mind is the main thing the world is trying to influence for its own gain. It's also your mind that God desires to renew daily so you can live in an intimate and abundant relationship with Him.

> *Do not conform to the pattern of this world, but be transformed by the renewing of your mind.*
> —Romans 12:2a

God makes it clear that conforming to the world and being transformed by the renewal of our minds are in direct opposition. Our minds are either being won and submitted to the Kingdom of God, or they're not. When we make room for the Holy Spirit to transform us, there is a reason He begins with our *minds*. Our biggest obstacle to transformation isn't that we don't behave right; it's that we don't believe the right things. Basically, we don't think right. But when we open our hearts and allow ourselves to be renewed by God's Word, we can finally overcome the thoughts that try to steal our peace, freedom and joy. This is why the Holy Spirit's first step is renewing our thinking with God's Word, and then our emotions and actions naturally begin to follow.

Here is one idea of how our usual belief and behavior cycle works:

1. First, there is some sort of event or trigger.
2. This triggers a thought (stemming from a core belief).
3. This triggers an emotion.
4. This leads us to respond or act.

If you've been in counseling, you may know this "flow" as cognitive behavioral therapy. In this style of therapy, the goal is to help clients become aware of their thoughts, emotions and beliefs, identify negative or inaccurate thinking, and reshape the negative thinking. Though this is a very old psychological approach, I would argue that God revealed it to us first through Scriptures like Romans 12:2!

There is also one thing I'd like to add that I have come to realize from past therapy sessions with clients and day-to-day conversations with friends. While it's true that our thoughts often trigger an emotion, I have also seen how sometimes our emotions come before the thought and can actually solidify certain beliefs. For example, "I feel lonely a lot, therefore I am unwanted," instead of "I am unwanted so I feel lonely."

As Lysa TerKeurst puts it, "Our feelings are indicators not dictators."[1] While emotions can indicate false beliefs and the true condition of our hearts, they were never meant to be relied upon for wise decision-making or belief formation. This is something to keep in mind to help you assess core beliefs, to notice your thought patterns and how your emotions play a role in your belief system.

Either way, we can be quick to bow down to our thoughts and emotions instead of pausing long enough to do some detective work. We must proactively take every thought captive and submit it under God's Word, Truth and authority (2 Corinthians 10:5). We can do this by asking questions like:

"Where did this thought come from?"
"Does this thought or belief align with God's Word?"
"What are my emotions possibly indicating?"
"Is this a false belief?"
"Will my behavior honor the Lord if I act on this belief?"

The more we do this, the more proactively and purposefully we can search God's Word so it can heal old wounds and transform old beliefs.

With that said, when you recognize a false belief, the first step is to surrender it to the Lord so He can renew your mind! Make your mind a disciple of His Word. Next, resist it by choosing to disagree with the false belief and countering the lie with truth found in Scripture. Remember, you have been given authority over your thinking. Your thoughts are something you *can* control! While you may not be able to control the automatic thoughts that pop up, you get to decide which thoughts stay, are rejected, or are renewed.

Think of it this way. If you are a hotel manager, while you cannot control who goes in and out of your lobby, you can control whom you give a room key. It's the same with your thoughts. You may not be able to control the automatic ones, but you can control what you chew on and what you spit out.

Friends, we have been given sound minds! With that said, we must engage our sound minds with a decision to think on truth, not the lie (2 Timothy 1:7 and Philippians 4:8). The more we get into God's Word, the more God's Word gets into us. Read it, study it, meditate on it and memorize it! The Holy Spirit then utilizes God's Word and uses it to transform our minds so that a new pattern emerges. As He does, what you will find is that the next time a life circumstance occurs, a new cycle emerges where *transformed* thinking brings *transformed* behaviors.

Notice Which Kingdom You're Mentally Set On

We may not think twice about which kingdom we mentally seek, but it has a huge influence on our beliefs. Our minds are ultimately servants to our spirit or our flesh, which seek two different things.

> *Since, then, you have been raised with Christ, set your hearts on things above, where Christ is, seated at the right hand of God. Set your minds on things above, not on earthly things.*
> —Colossians 3:1–2

> *But seek first his kingdom and his righteousness, and all these things will be given to you as well.*
> —Matthew 6:33

Before coming to Christ, we had old natures (old mindsets) ruled by the earthly kingdom. Our earthly mindsets believed the lies of the world, conformed to the values of the world, and were mentally distracted by the cares of the world.

When we are in Christ, we are new creations with new natures ruled by a Kingdom mindset. This means we believe the truth of God's Word, pursue what God says is rewarded in His Kingdom, and stop chasing after worldly things.

Which kingdom would you say you mentally seek more? When we mentally set our minds on things above, we are able to live and behave as God's holy people here on earth. If we want to live as children of God, following His way and doing all things for His glory, we need to let go of our old beliefs (old natures) and put on the new beliefs (new natures).

Abide in the Truth

And you will know the truth, and the truth will set you free.
—John 8:32 (New Living Testament)

But when he, the Spirit of truth, comes, he will guide you into all the truth. He will not speak on his own; he will speak only what he hears.
—John 16:13

Jesus was clear that knowing the truth sets us free. Free from our old beliefs, old behaviors, old habits and old lies. The Truth has to be accepted in our minds before it can be hidden in our hearts and represented by our actions. If our minds and beliefs are not also abiding in God and His Truth, transformation is impossible. Abiding in God's Truth with our minds means our thoughts and beliefs are continuously connected, reliant on God's Word. Staying reliant on God's Word is a daily choice to see the Bible as a trustworthy source of information that you believe *over* your own senses or others' opinions.

Sometimes we struggle to understand God's Word. As a follower of Jesus, you have the Spirit of Truth with you and within you, helping you believe, understand and rejoice in the Bible. It takes both your willingness to know the Truth and the Holy Spirit's power to help you understand and live that Truth. Therefore, you must be in God's Word daily so you can give the Holy Spirit something to work with! I encourage you to start small. I know it can feel overwhelming trying to think about how to begin reading God's Word. The good news is that you aren't meant to understand it by your own strength! The Holy Spirit is there to guide and teach you.

One great way to start is picking a book in the Bible (I recommend the Gospel of John in the New Testament or the Book of Psalms). Commit to a few verses every day. Journal them. Yes, write them down! There is something about doodling and writing that taps into the creative part of our brain and helps us then dwell even more deeply on what we are reading. You don't have to journal forever, but it's a great way to stay focused as you start. If you're looking for a commentary to help you go a little deeper (which I would only use *after* you've given the Holy Spirit time to teach you one on one), I enjoy the Enduring Word Commentary online.

Now is a great time to start. Today can be the day you sit down and reveal false beliefs that don't match God's Word. If you are unwilling, not only will you continue to be frustrated with your lack of spiritual growth, but you will also be more vulnerable to the enemy and his schemes.

Set your thoughts on the things of God. Meditate on what is true, honorable, just, pure, lovely, commendable, worthy of praise, and of excellence (Philippians 4:8). Start each day by setting your mind on the character of the living God and your new identity in Christ. As you allow God's Word to be the foundation of your thought life, your mind will be won for the Kingdom! The negative thoughts, false beliefs and insecurities you come against daily will flee from you in the glorious light of God's truth and grace. This is God's promise for you and me every day. This will change your behaviors and responses toward yourself and the world around you.

HEALTHY IN BODY

Our beliefs shape our realities. That includes the reality of our health. We are more likely to engage in health-promoting behaviors like exercising and proper nutrition if we have the right beliefs.

Going back to the cycle of beliefs and behaviors, oftentimes we allow our emotions to fuel false beliefs, which result in poor choices in behavior. For example, maybe you had a difficult day and gave in to emotional eating *(life circumstances)*. Because of this, you feel angry, hopeless and defeated *(feelings)*. Therefore, you conclude you'll never find freedom with food *(feelings have created beliefs)*. You then stop trying to make any effort to practice self-control with food *(behaviors)*. You will live out what you believe. Therefore, if you believe you will never find freedom with food, you will stay trapped in those negative emotions and behaviors. It's really hard to arrive at an outcome you've deemed impossible. With God, friend, all things are possible (Matthew 19:26).

In chapter 1 (*His Way > My Way*), we learned that denial of self is the only way to discover our true selves in Christ. This is just as relevant to our beliefs. To take care of our bodies with God, His way and for His glory, we must be willing to deny our old thought patterns, false beliefs, and even our emotions. They have no place on the throne of our hearts. This impacts how and why we care for our temporary "tents."

What changed the way I took care of my body wasn't trying harder (*behavior modification*) but thinking right (*mind and heart transformation*). Before I cooperated with the Holy Spirit's desire to renew my mind to help me see my body and health through God's eyes, I was stuck in my way. I didn't believe who I was in Christ, and it reflected in how I treated myself and my body. I was obsessed with exercise and addicted to food. Though I "tried" to stop, secretly I didn't want to stop. Why? Because of my beliefs. My false beliefs and pride delayed my healing. I didn't want to admit I was wrong and that "my way" got me lost.

Thankfully, God relentlessly pursues our hearts. When I finally humbled myself to admit I was lost and my beliefs were misguided, transformation could begin. With that said, I would like to share with you eight things I wish I had *believed* before I started taking care of my health in 2008. Some of them are familiar from previous chapters, but it will be helpful to revisit them again here now that you are even deeper into your journey. It's amazing how we can hear the same thing twice and see a whole new meaning the second time! Not because the truth changed but because we are being transformed. I am certain these beliefs would have produced a completely different reality for my health.

My body isn't mine.
This seems simple, but sometimes it's the most simple truths we struggle most to believe and live out. My body is not mine; I know this now. Ten years ago was another story. I lived and treated my body like it was mine to do with as I pleased, for my own gain. I never talked to God about it. I didn't think He cared, and I thought I knew better (ridiculous, I know).

I wish I could go back and say, "Actually, it's not yours. God made it. He owns it. You're the steward of it." As we've addressed before, we were created through Christ and for Christ (Colossians 1:15–16). Our bodies are made by Him and for Him. This belief changes how we see, use and take care of our bodies!

My body isn't my enemy.
It's so easy to abuse, misuse, hate, resist and condemn our bodies. It takes more self-control, patience and grace to love them and care for them well. The more we can see our bodies as gifts given by God to be stewarded, rather than as problems that need to be fixed, the better we can partner with our bodies to keep them healthy and strong.

My body isn't my identity.
Health and wellness only get complicated when we put our identity in them. God created us in a way where we can only find significance from Him. Any other path we try to take

to find contentment will leave us with the same outcome: disappointment.

Even though I had always known what the Bible said about me, I either did not care or did not believe it *more* than what others said about me or what I thought about myself. Step one for me was to pray and ask the Lord to help me care more about what He said than what I or the world said. I asked Him to help me align my thoughts and beliefs with His Word. This changed how I read the Bible. The next step was to live it out by the power of the Holy Spirit. Once we solidify our identities in Christ, we can put health and wellness in their proper place. We don't idolize our health or neglect it; we just care for it well and move on!

My body is temporary.
Because this was *not* my belief, I lived like my body was the main thing, and it consumed my mind. What I ate consumed my mind. How much I worked out consumed my mind. My body became a distraction to my main purpose the moment I started caring more about it than Jesus. Our bodies are temporary tents. Really think about this! When we store up our treasures in our bodies, they are meaningless in the light of eternity.

I had to learn that my body was not the main thing. But while it wasn't the main thing, it could help me *do* the main thing. What is the main thing? To delight in the Lord, magnify Him and spread the gospel! We are here to prepare the way for Jesus's second return, to love God, love people and spread the gospel. My body is either going to enhance my ability to live out this purpose or limit it.

When we set our minds on what is eternal, we can steward what we are given on earth without worrying or becoming consumed by it. Ultimately, I had to redefine my "why" for health. It was not to get skinny or sexy (anymore). Instead, it was to glorify the Lord and serve others. As much as it depended on me, I didn't want my body to become a barrier to anything He called me to do.

My body responds to my thoughts and beliefs toward it.
It sounds weird to say, "Your body can hear you," but it can. What we believe will come out in what we say and how we live. There have actually been scientific studies that show how our cells respond to what we say! This one might be a fun Google rabbit hole (after you finish this chapter, of course!).

Therefore, I had to ask the Lord to renew my mind and help me retrain my words so I spoke life over my body. My body is supposed to be another way I worship the Lord! How can I honor God with my body if I am constantly speaking negatively toward it?

> *Pleasant words are a honeycomb; sweet to the soul and healing to the bones.*
> —Proverbs 16:24

> *Death and life are in the power of the tongue, and those who love it will eat its fruits.*
> — Proverbs 18:21

This Scripture absolutely also applies to the way you speak to yourself. I had to learn how to speak life over myself and my body, to honor it rather than condemn it. If you want to learn how to have loving thoughts toward your body, look no further than the famously known "love chapter" in 1 Corinthians 13:4–6. If you want to experience love, joy, peace, forbearance, kindness, goodness, faithfulness, gentleness and self-control toward your body, it won't take willpower but the Holy Spirit's power (Galatians 5:22–23). If you want to have positive thoughts toward your body, remember Philippians 4:8. I am purposefully only citing the scripture! I encourage you to have your Bible out and open (or your Bible app ready) to look up these scriptures yourself. I promise it's because I love you and not to inconvenience you. You won't regret reading His Word yourself!

Have you ever applied those scriptures to your body? God did not make us only as spiritual beings. Scripture addresses our spirit, mind and body.

The way we talk to ourselves matters. Let's commit to biblical self-talk, which helps us change our thinking to align with God's Truth. Biblical self-talk is Christ-honoring, good for our souls, beneficial to our spiritual growth, and profitable for our service to others. Where is biblical self-talk most needed when it comes to your body and health journey?

My body will go through seasons.
Why was that so hard for me to accept? I remember when I would get so frustrated every time my body would leave a "sweet spot" in weight or size. The reality is, our bodies, hormones and metabolisms will change. It's totally normal for our bodies to change. Everyone around you has a body that will change too, for different reasons!

Forcing our bodies to perform the same way in all seasons is simply not realistic or fair. So, what if instead we anticipate the change and reevaluate our goals and expectations to match what our bodies currently can do? I bet we would get frustrated a whole lot less and be less likely to go to extremes!

In my pregnancy, I knew my body was going to gain weight. Its job was to house another human! The extra care resulted in that gain I saw. That wasn't a license for me to stop caring and neglect it, nor was it a license for me to be so consumed by the weight gain that I lost all joy. When I kept the right purpose in mind behind caring for my body, I was able to still show up, move it, nourish it, rest it, and stretch it consistently. If I was going to gain either way, I would much rather have been gaining and have energy, strength and stamina than gaining and feeling fatigued and weak.

When we live in the past, we get depressed. We get stuck thinking about how our bodies used to be, how we used to feel, and the clothes we used to be able to wear. I'm encouraging you today to focus instead on the body you have now. The more you do this, the harder it will be to get stuck passively accepting your body, and the easier it will become to proactively steward it with joy and peace.

My body is unique.
All of our bodies are different. I remember when I would try so hard to force my body into a certain shape and would be willing to try any approach recommended to make it happen. But something that works for someone else may not always work for you.

I tried so many different approaches and was never consistent because all I wanted was weight loss. I jumped from "wagon" to "wagon." If I could go back thirteen years, I would question my 2008 self and say, "If weight loss was not a goal—if you were already at your goal weight range or for some reason could never lose weight—would you actually pick this path for your health? Would you deem this approach wise, sustainable and sensible for you?" Talk about a motive check!

I've had to learn to be cautious about what path I choose to care for my body. I have to consider if the path will hinder or enhance my life and whether or not it will be right for *my* body. This is my usual process now before deciding on any new approach for the care of my body:

- First, I talk to God about it.
- Second, I do the research. I try to learn about the science of how this approach will benefit my body. I ask questions like: Has there been enough research done? Does the person launching it have a degree in this area? I look at studies and testimonials. I look for extremes (which I try to avoid). I also like to ask a few friends that are registered dieticians to listen to their thoughts.
- Third, I ask a few questions like: Can I sustain it? Does it make sense for me? Will it enhance or hinder my life? Are the sacrifices required worth it, or will it complicate things for my family and me? Will it steal joy from living in the present? Does it bend toward extremes?

I hope you find these questions as helpful to you as they are to me!

My body needs food and rest.
Again, so simple, and yet I never rested and I was scared to eat. I overcomplicated nutrition because diet culture overcomplicated

it. I was so desperate to control the outcome of my health that I saw rest days as a weakness and a delay from my goals.

Struggling to rest is often an indication of a lack of trust in God's ability to sustain our efforts. At least it was for me! I had to address the heart issue behind fear of rest days and let God renew my mind to help me see rest as productive, purposeful and powerful. Rest reduced my risk of injury, improved my performance, prevented muscle fatigue, and kept me reliant on God's grace.

In addition to rest, our bodies need food and nutrients to function well. Say it with me: "My body needs food." For some of you, this is obvious. For others, this is a truth you have yet to receive, and maybe today is the day you finally receive it. Food gets complicated when we misuse it as a source of comfort, control, companionship or security. But when we focus on fueling without reckless restriction or extreme deprivation, we can put food back in its proper place.

As you can see, while it's great to tackle behavioral changes in your health, it is wiser to start by identifying your beliefs and how they influence the habits you've created. New ideas never last when you try to force them into an old mindset. We can't get new results with false beliefs and old behaviors. Our beliefs shape our habits. Our habits will either help or hurt our bodies, which will either enhance or hinder the *main thing* we're called to do.

Right now God longs to meet with you and heal the wounds, lies and insecurities that have kept you from loving yourself and others well. Run to Him with open arms and allow Him to do a mighty work in you today!

One practical step you can take today is to start a journal specific to your wellness journey. In this journal, I want you to identify one lie you've been believing about yourself and your body that has been shaping your life. Do you believe your body is made through Christ and for Christ? Do you believe you are His workmanship, fearfully and wonderfully made, His child? Do you believe that caring for your body is another way to glorify Him and enhance your capacity to serve others? The more you identify the false beliefs, surrender them, and replace them with Truth, the less complacency, pride and striving become a temptation in your health journey.

I especially want you to revisit this journal entry in your low times when emotions are loudest and it's hardest to remember the truth. Flip back to your journal entry and meditate on what is true and say "no!" to unconstructive and negative thoughts that go against what Philippians 4:8 instructs you to think on. I am rooting for you!

PRAYER

Father, You alone can transform minds and heal hearts. Thank You for Your perfect love that casts out every fear and every lie. Please soften my heart to not only know the Truth but believe it and live it. Show me the lies I have been believing that have prevented me from fully trusting You. Please help me put an end to the connections in my brain that are tied to my old way of thinking and form new pathways with Your Word and Truth. Help me receive and believe the fullness of Your love for me that will enable me to love myself and those around me with Your kind of love. I love You. Amen.

REFLECT

❶ Where do you need God to do a mighty work in your beliefs today? Ask the Spirit to reveal what areas He wants to heal today. Ask Him to guide you to a false belief or insecurity He longs to speak to with His truth and love.

❷ Which of the eight beliefs about the body shared in the "Healthy in Body" section do you need to meditate on most today?

....
....
....
....
....
....
....
....
....
....
....
....
....

❸ Take out that journal and write down one lie you've been believing about yourself and your body that has been shaping your life. Then, disarm it with what God says.

....
....
....
....
....
....
....
....
....
....
....

GRACE > GUILT

*W*hen you make a mistake or fall into sin, is your reflex to run to God or run from Him? One of the traps I believe we can easily fall into is making the things we've done (past regrets, recent failures) bigger than what Jesus has done for us on the cross. We make our weaknesses bigger than God's grace.

In my own experience, I have learned that we are usually motivated by grace or guilt. Guilt can indeed motivate, but its motivation leads to restless striving as we attempt to save and redeem ourselves. Grace, however, motivates us to greater dependence on God, His love and mercy.

In this chapter, we will uncover the depth and healing power of God's grace, while understanding the difference between conviction and condemnation.

STRONG IN SPIRIT

One of the ways guilt can creep into our lives is through the word "should:"

"I *should* be exercising more."

"I *should've* eaten better."

"I *should* try harder."

"I *should* be seeing faster results."

"I *should* weigh less."

"I *should*..."

The "should" bunny trail can make an appearance in our marriages, parenting, careers, ministries and health. It complicates what was once simple. It burdens what was once light. It's a heavy word that leaves us heavy. The question we must ask before acting upon this chain of thinking is, "*Who* is the voice behind the '*should*'?"

The source is one of two things: the Holy Spirit or Satan. One comes to convict with grace, truth and love; the other comes to accuse with deceit, guilt and shame. I want to briefly explain the difference before diving into the topic of grace.

Conviction

The Holy Spirit's mission in our lives is to make us more like Christ. To do so, He counsels, corrects, convicts, comforts, helps, and leads us in Truth.

We, like sheep, often go astray. When we do, we have the loving Shepherd right there, using His rod and staff to bring us back to Himself. Guilt, then, is an emotion that can stir within our hearts when we are doing something that is not bringing us closer to Christ and interrupting our abiding in Him.

I want to be clear that guilt is not God's voice; conviction is. Guilt is simply an emotion like happiness or sadness. Emotions aren't bad; they simply aren't always true, and therefore should never be in the "driver's seat" of our lives. Emotions help reveal what's going on internally, but they were never meant to lead what we do externally. Therefore, the emotion of guilt, if explored with God, can reveal conviction. Conviction is when the Holy Spirit reveals sin in our lives and moves us to repentance.

> When he [Holy Spirit] comes, he will prove the world to be in the wrong about sin and righteousness and judgment.
> —John 16:8

Conviction is a two-step process. First, the Holy Spirit reveals our sin to us. Second, He shows us how to turn from it so we can walk in righteousness instead. As we see in 2 Corinthians 5:21, "*God made him who had no sin to be sin for us, so that in him we might become the righteousness of God.*" The Holy Spirit convicts us in an effort to call us *up* to the righteousness we have been given in Christ.

Without an awareness of our sin, we will not appreciate God's grace. We can glance at the *emotion* of guilt to determine if there is conviction within it and if confession and repentance are needed. If it is condemning guilt, we can quickly dismantle it with God's Word, the Truth.

Condemnation

Because guilt and conviction can often seem so similar, Satan relies on our own confusion and uncertainty to trip us up. Satan wants us to wallow in guilt and shame. One of his top goals is to discourage us about the progress we are making in our walks with God and leave us doubting the truth of our identity, salvation and security.

While Satan can't create new ideas in us, he *can* manipulate them. He often tugs on the emotions, flesh desires and insecurities already within us to see if we take the bait of doubting God's love and grace or minimizing His holiness.

Satan has many methods to his schemes, which we are warned of in Ephesians 6. One of his most common methods is accusation. Accusation leaves us:

- Beating ourselves up
- Repeating mistakes
- Scared to run to God
- Forgetting God's love
- Identifying ourselves with our decisions (I made a bad choice; therefore, *I am* bad)
- Making every effort to try to save ourselves

Each of those outcomes is an indication that it's the enemy working and not the Holy Spirit.

Which Is It?

Unlike conviction, the ultimate goal of condemning guilt is to make us believe and feel as worthless, loveless and hopeless as possible. Conviction's purpose is to restore our fellowship with Christ, and its way is paved by grace and marked by peace.

Conviction prompts us to draw closer to God to receive His forgiveness.
Condemnation prompts us to hide from Him in shame.

Conviction leads to breakthrough and change.
Condemnation paralyzes and leaves us broken.

Conviction leads to surrender.
Condemnation leads to striving.

Conviction drives us to greater dependence on God.
Condemnation drives us to independence from God.

With this in mind, after asking, "Who is the voice behind the thought?" the next question is, "Does this thought keep my gaze on the cross and move me closer to Jesus, or does it leave me wanting to run and hide in shame?" Your gaze and direction will reveal whether it's conviction or condemnation.

Grace

One of my favorite moments in the Bible where we see grace in action is how Peter responds to seeing Jesus after His resurrection and after he has denied Him three times. I encourage you to open your Bible to John 21 to read the whole story.

I can only imagine the deep sense of guilt and shame that could have overtaken Peter the same way it did for Judas (the man who betrayed Jesus). After Jesus rose from the grave, the disciples had been eagerly waiting to see Him. I am not sure how long they were waiting or when each of the occurrences exactly happened. What I do know is that all of a sudden, Peter decided to go fishing, which seems like a regression for him, considering that was the career he had left behind three years previous to follow Jesus. Nevertheless, he went, and so did a few of the other disciples.

After some time with no luck catching fish, Jesus appeared and gave them instructions on where to cast their net. They did not know yet that it was Jesus. The moment Peter *did* recognize that it *was* Jesus, "He wrapped his outer garment around him (for he had taken it off) and jumped into the water" (John 21:7b).

Peter jumped into the water and ran *to* Jesus. He didn't hide. He didn't run away. He didn't get numb and say, "Forget it; what's the point?" Peter had finally come to really know who Jesus was, and he was received by and with grace. This account in John 21 gives us immense hope. It gives us confidence that our failures don't put us out of reach of Jesus's saving and restorative grace. There is reconciliation and restoration—the two things grace does.

I think for many of us, we find that grace is a gift we don't know how to receive. We are so used to the world's systems of earning and performing, which makes grace a concept hard to grasp. Yet, it's grace alone that has the power to transform lives and bring freedom to the captives. It's by grace alone that we are saved. Therefore, what better way to redeem our time than to consistently and passionately pursue a greater revelation of God's grace?

> *Therefore no one will be declared righteous in God's sight by the works of the law; rather, through the law we become conscious of our sin. But now apart from the law the righteousness of God has been made known, to which the Law and the Prophets testify. This righteousness is given through faith in Jesus Christ to all who believe. There is no difference between Jew and Gentile, for all have sinned and fall short of the glory of God, and all are justified freely by his grace through the redemption that came by Christ Jesus.*
>
> —Romans 3:20–24

Notice a few things in this passage:

- We can't earn or perform our way to achieve righteousness.
- Through the law we become conscious of our sin, which allows us to resist it or confess it.
- Apart from the law, righteousness has been made known.
- Righteousness is given through faith in Jesus to all who believe.
- All have sinned and fallen short of the glory of God.
- All are justified freely by His grace through the redemption that came by Christ.

Ultimately, grace says Jesus has done all that we cannot, and He is the salvation and hope for all. Grace doesn't minimize the cross; it magnifies it. The more we remain aware of being *both* sinners and also *loved* children in Christ, the more we will grow in grace.

Since grace is freely given to us in Jesus, it can't be taken away later when we stumble or fall. We can be honest with ourselves and God and confess our sins because of what Jesus Christ has done on the cross. God reminds us that Jesus has paid the price for our sin and that His grace is ever ready to meet us and to minister to our insufficiencies (see 2 Corinthians 12:9). God then sends us back into the world with the words, *"Go and sin no more"* (John 8:11).

Remember, God's grace isn't a license for us to keep living according to our flesh (our way) but gives us the power to live by the Spirit (*His* way)!

Grace is God's love and favor in action, and it's sufficient for you and me right now. Yes, right now. Not someday. Not when we get our act together. It's sufficient at this moment. God didn't tell Paul, "My grace will be sufficient for you when..." or that "It is sufficient *for now.*" No, it is sufficient to cover our past, present and future.

When I stop and meditate on God's character, I find myself wanting to burst with gratitude and praise. When I fall short, He covers the distance. When I am doubting, He loves me still. When I am struggling to draw near, He remains present. He doesn't leave. He doesn't condemn. He doesn't stop loving me.

The same is true for you. When we come to really know Him, we will never allow guilt to paralyze us again. Instead, we will leap out of the boat like Peter, running to the Father. He is our rest and our home.

Whatever you are currently wrestling with as you read this, you are invited to rest in God's grace and become completely dependent on it in this very moment and forever after that. Rise up with me, friend, and praise Him for His grace, rest in His grace, depend on His grace, and be motivated by His grace!

HEALTHY IN BODY

The Fruitless Cycle of Guilt

There's a reason why in each chapter we always begin with *Strong in Spirit* before we get to *Healthy in Body.* God's Word and Truth should saturate our very being and change how we do *everything,* including taking care of our bodies. I have no doubt you have experienced guilt throughout your wellness journey. Guilt is a powerful emotion, and we've learned (or been told) to use it as a motivator, which rarely works. If it does, not only is its path miserable, it's short-lived and often destructive.

The fruitless cycle of guilt and shame can sometimes look like this:

- You choose to eat something that is not beneficial to your body and beat yourself up about it.
- You then either punish yourself by working out twice as hard (or long) to make up for it, don't eat the rest of the day, or call the day a wash and eat everything in sight.
- Next thing you know, the cycle repeats itself the next day.

The reality is, we aren't always going to get it right. Many of us still struggle with the flesh when it comes to idolatry, selfishness, pride, envy, and even gluttony. Instead of avoiding, minimizing or denying our sin, let's quickly, humbly and honestly confess and repent as we ask God to forgive and restore us.

Conviction moves our gaze toward the cross, enabling us to confess, repent and turn because of God's grace. Facing our flesh in the area of our health becomes another training ground for the Holy Spirit to renew us as He makes us more like Christ.

There is also another side to our struggles. Sometimes we overlook our human limits. When we do, we set standards and expectations for ourselves to strive for that are unrealistic, unsustainable and unnecessary. Even worse, we try to meet those very expectations with our willpower, which is often sourced by guilt.

The Perfection Infection

There is no such thing as a perfect body or a perfect health journey. We will all struggle with making mistakes, skipping workouts, and making poor decisions with nutrition. If our bodies become the main thing we are pursuing instead of Jesus Himself (who *is* the Main Thing), we will overmagnify the stumbling in our health journey to the point where it consumes our mind more than God's Word.

What if instead, when we give in to our flesh and stumble, we run to Jesus, thank Him for His grace, ask Him to use the trial to make us more like Him, and praise Him for the remaining hours of that very day where we can make the next best choice?

Spiral Up

While guilt keeps us in a downward spiral, grace enables us to spiral up. No matter how many poor choices you've made today, you can choose to spiral up in the next one. How? Maybe you spiral up by drinking more water instead of soda or coffee the rest of the day. Maybe you add more vegetables to your plate with dinner. Maybe you speak with compassion over yourself rather than condemning, or you're proactive instead of passive, or you surrender control instead of striving for it. If you desire to make the next best choice, I am confident the Holy Spirit will enable you to do it.

Remove the blanket of guilt, friend. If the emotion of guilt is not quickly submitted and surrendered to the Lord, it can consume your mind and control your life with "have tos" and "shoulds." It will keep you reliant on yourself in a downward spiral of striving or quitting, and defining yourself by your choices instead of who God says you are.

God's Grace Meets Us in Our Weakness

God is the Chain Breaker. He is the Miracle Worker. He is the Way Maker. He longs to renew us and satisfy us with His love as we experience His abounding grace. We don't have the power to renew our own minds or heal our own hearts. What we can do is come to the Lord—weary, weak and honest—trusting that He is our rest and strength.

It starts with honesty with God. God doesn't want our perfection or our striving. He wants us to be honest about our weaknesses so we can be wholehearted in our surrender. That's one key to really experiencing the depths of His grace. What you'll discover is that grace is a more life-giving, heart-fulfilling and spirit-strengthening motivator than shame or guilt ever can be.

God's grace is sufficient. You don't need to work for His grace but simply be available to receive it and let it change you. His grace is what will enable you to make the next best choice. While guilt may be a strong emotion, the good news is that grace is an unchanging, unearned and unfailing Truth. It is sufficient because Christ's death on the cross was sufficient. Grace moves us from "I have to work out and nourish my body well" to "I get to work out and nourish my body well." Grace keeps our eyes up and our knees bowed down.

I encourage you to meditate on God's love, the cross, and His power in you today. Acknowledge if there is anything in your wellness journey that requires confession and repentance and then ask the Holy Spirit to help you make the next best choice (spiral up) with His power and grace. He is with you and for you.

Make room for the Holy Spirit to fill you, enable you, and set you free because of His great love and sufficient grace.

PRAYER

Father, thank You for Your immeasurable, unqualified and sufficient grace. Through Jesus, You extend Your grace to me, and it's by Your grace that I have been saved. I did nothing to earn Your love and yet You still love me. You have forgiven my sins and removed them from me. Thank You for this amazing grace! Today I ask that You lead me by Your Holy Spirit and keep me from straying to the right or the left. By Your grace, help me make the next right and holy choice and refuse to make a decision contrary to Your way. Help me to comprehend Your grace more and more in my life. I love You. Amen.

REFLECT

❶ In what ways are you living a guilt-driven life? Where do you need a fresh vision for living by grace?

....
....
....
....
....
....
....

❷ Ask the Holy Spirit to give you a fresh vision of how deeply God's grace goes in any and every circumstance you face. Ask Him to fill you with a fresh revelation of how deeply He loves you regardless of what you do. Allow Him to lead you into a lifestyle of living by grace in every pursuit, relationship, thought and perspective.

....
....
....
....
....
....
....
....
....
....
....
....
....
....

❸ How can you spiral up today in your wellness as you choose to be motivated by grace?

....
....
....
....
....
....
....
....

HIS WAY = THE WAY

A Personal Message

I am filled with all kinds of emotions as I write this final chapter. I am so thankful for God's grace. This book would not have been possible if it were not for His redeeming power in my own life. You must know that in my past, I chose every single "less than" option you see in every chapter and was left with a massive knot in my health and heart. But God. While Satan tried to convince me it was too tangled up to be fixed, the Holy Spirit came close to remind me that God can redeem anything.

I love the reminder we have from Psalm 34:19: "The righteous person may have many troubles, but the Lord delivers him from them *all*." (emphasis added)

What encouragement! All means all, friend! The big, small, seen, unseen; in the one-and-done struggle and in the one that keeps coming back. He is with you, for you, and able to deliver you.

Every chapter is a journey I am still on with the Lord. I pray you choose to walk with Him in it as well. If, like me, you have a past that feels broken beyond repair, may you be encouraged. God doesn't waste pain, waiting or even failure. The cross not only covers current and future sin but also our past regrets. May this truth drive us faster to our knees, worship, humble gratitude, and determination to love God more than anything else.

Remember the Truth

I remember when I started exploring all the ways God's way is upside down from the world, it seemed like I could write forever. But really, everything we need to know has already been written by God Himself in His Word.

This is why this book isn't necessarily filled with new ideas. My priority was simply to remind you of what God has already said and empower you to live it out with Him and for Him. My prayer is that each chapter points you back to Jesus and reminds you that no area of your life is too small or irrelevant for His power and glory to shine through, not even your body.

In total transparency, I've wondered if a book called *Wellness His Way* would even be necessary if we are fully submitting ourselves to being humbly led by the Holy Spirit in *every* part of our lives. Confusion and complications disappear when God is the foundation, focus and point of our lives.

We complicate our wellness (or anything really) when we either try to do it apart from God or we place it above God.

End the *And*

It's time to end the trend of Jesus *and* ___ (you can fill in the blanks with whatever else you are tempted to pursue in addition to Jesus or even more than Jesus). Nowhere in Scripture do we see that we can choose two masters. Matthew 6:24 says, *"No one can serve two masters. Either you will hate the one and love the other, or you will be devoted to the one and despise the other."*

We cannot live God's way partially, halfheartedly or with mediocrity. Interestingly, when it comes to health and wellness, I would tell you that "all or nothing" is a horrible mindset to have. A step is better than no step. Yet in our faith, it really is all or nothing. We either pursue holiness or we don't. It's either we follow Jesus or we don't. It's either we are hot or cold. There is no lukewarm. There is no "a little Jesus" and "a little me." It's either Jesus is everything in my life, or I've said "no" to His authority in my life.

Christine Cain said it well: "We keep trying to add Jesus to our nets instead of dropping our nets entirely to follow Him."[1] Jesus' disciples immediately dropped their nets, their source of security and perhaps even identity, and followed Jesus completely. There was no Plan B. What is preventing us from living this way? What are the nets we are still holding onto, even if only by our pinkies?

It takes radical effort and intention to ensure daily that Jesus is our greatest reward. We must daily preach the gospel to ourselves, surrender all we have and all we do to the Lord, lay down our wills for His, and set our minds on things above. Living His way means waking up every day and dying to ourselves and offering our lives and bodies as a living sacrifice. In Romans 12:2, Paul says, *"Do not conform to the pattern of this world, but be transformed by the renewing of your mind. Then you will be able to test and approve what God's will is—his good, pleasing and perfect will."*

As we partner with the Holy Spirit in the renewal of our minds as we spend time in God's Word, we will know God's will for our lives. This includes every part of our lives, even our health choices.

If we step back for a moment, we will discover that the answer to every temptation, every trial, every struggle is Jesus. Being content in Jesus, captivated by Jesus, and satisfied with Jesus is the journey we must pursue.

I would like to invite you to open up to Psalm 119: 57–60 as we close out our journey together, and read it out loud with me:

"You are my portion, Lord; I have promised to obey Your words. I have sought Your face with all my heart; be gracious to me according to Your promise. I have considered my ways and have turned my steps to Your statutes. I will hasten and not delay to obey Your commands."

God Is to Be Our Portion

While in some cases portion means "ration," in Hebrew the psalmist is declaring God to be his inheritance and future. When we have Jesus, we have everything.

I think it's safe to assume that you have set many goals in your life. Maybe your goal is to get up earlier, so you put more effort into going to bed earlier. Maybe your goal is to be on social media less, so you set strong boundaries with your phone and turn all notifications off. Our goals influence our actions.

When reading this psalm, I cannot help but pause and consider: Is God my goal? Is God the main thing that I really want in this life, and are my actions lining up with that? Our gaze influences our chase. Meaning what we gaze upon, we will pursue.

How would your life change if Jesus was your gaze?
How would your pursuit of health change if Jesus was your gaze?
How would your "hustle" change if Jesus was your gaze?

When we are satisfied in Christ, we stop trying to find satisfaction in the pursuit of fleshly things. Suddenly, all the things the enemy attempts to use to distract, dissatisfy and discourage us lose their power and hold over us. Something like taking care of our bodies no longer requires this wrestling, confusion or overwhelm we feel. It's just another area in which we get to seek Jesus with all our hearts, walk with Him, and become like Him.

Friend, the most precious gift that God has given you as a Believer is Himself. By grace, God forgives, pardons and accepts you not based on what you have done, but based on the work of Jesus alone and received by you through faith alone. Forgiveness makes a way for His most precious gift, which is union, communion and fellowship with Him.

May our greatest reward, desire and treasure be Jesus. If we strive toward anything, let's strive to ensure that nothing else occupies our hearts as the ultimate object of our affection; that God is the ultimate object of our affection. Like the psalmist, may we grow to boldly declare, *"You are my portion, Lord,"* because we are so satisfied in Christ and with Christ.

Consider Your Ways and Turn

Spending time in God's Word always provokes self-examination and transformation. The more we see God clearly, the better we will recognize what in our life is not aligned with His Word. To do all things with God, His way and for His glory, requires an honest consideration of our ways. This includes the way we think, act, speak and ultimately live. Are we thinking, speaking, acting and ultimately living the way Jesus would? Let's make it our aim to humble ourselves and turn from whatever is in us that remains to be focused on self rather than God.

Finally, let us hasten to obey. Yes, hasten! It's true that haste is reckless and dangerous when we are running our race our way. Yet, immediate obedience is never reckless when we are running the race marked out for us by God and relying on His power and grace.

Never Forget the Main Thing

I want to remind you a final time that our bodies are not the main thing. Our mission here is to prepare the way for Jesus's second coming. If anything becomes a distraction from the main thing, we are missing it. So, let's take care of our bodies in an effort to strengthen and support them so they can help us do the main thing. But may we never make our bodies themselves the main thing and fall into idolatry, worshiping the creation rather than the Creator Himself.

Do the things that are beneficial and enhance your body's strength, stamina and overall function.

Move your body with joy.
Nourish your body with purpose.
Rest your body with peace.

All those are wonderful things and allow us to honor God with the body He has given us. We get to offer it back to Him by stewarding the gift and glorifying the Giver. Find a plan for your fitness and wellness that will keep you intentional and serve you, not deplete you. Find accountability that will keep your eyes on the main thing and will call you up when you forget. Choose a nutrition approach that doesn't deprive, restrict or overwhelm you. Focus on eating what God has made regularly and what He didn't make occasionally. Stop living as a slave to your body and instead offer your body as a living sacrifice unto the Lord; use it for His purpose and glory!

Remember Corinthians 6:19–20. Let's read this one out loud too (there is such power in speaking Scripture out loud!):

"Do you not know that your bodies are temples of the Holy Spirit, who is in you, whom you have received from God? You are not your own; you were bought at a price. Therefore honor God with your bodies."

It honors God when we take care of our bodies, not when we obsess over them or neglect them. Let's take care of them with Him, His way, and for His glory.

Choose His way with me, friend. Choose:

Purpose > Preference
Creator > Creation
Stewardship > Ownership
Grace > Guilt
Beliefs > Behavior
Holiness > Freedom
Godfidence > Confidence
Obedience > Outcome
Growth focused > Goal focused
With God > For God
Faith > Fear
Humility > Pride
Honor Your Body > Accept Your Body
Discipline > Motivation

As you read over all the titles and concepts discussed in this book, I encourage you to reflect on which one was most helpful for you. Which one did your heart really need for healing to begin? I encourage you to go share what you learned with a friend or go journal about the themes that most stood out. Both actions will help you commit to memory what you learned, thus making it easier to recall and apply.

I am in His race with you and am rooting for you. If you only remember one theme in this book, I pray it is that we *get* to need God. We *get* to depend on Him. We *get* to glorify Him. We *get* to honor Him with our bodies. Let us joyfully steward what He has given us. May we become fully reliant on His power and grace to make us able as we remain available, willing and obedient.

NOTES

Before You Read

1. Keller, Timothy. *Counterfeit Gods: The Empty Promises of Money, Sex, and Power, and the Only Hope That Matters.* New York: Dutton, 2009. Print.

1 – His Way > My Way

1. Ogden, Greg. *Discipleship Essentials: A Guide To Building Your Life.* Downers Grove: InterVarsity Press, 2018. Print.
2. Myers, Michelle. She Works His Way workshop.
3. Ogden, *Discipleship Essentials.*

2 – Creator > Creation

1. Myers, Michelle. *Famous In Heaven & At Home: A 31–Day Character Study of the Proverbs 31 Woman.* 2016. Print.
2. Piper, John. "God Is Most Glorified In Us When We Are Most Satisfied In Him." *desiringGod*, 13 October 2012. <https://www.desiringgod.org/messages/god–is–most–glorified–in–us–when–we–are–most–satisfied–in–him>

3 – Stewardship > Ownership

1. Lewis, C.S. *Mere Christianity.* New York: Macmillan Publishing Co., Inc, 1960. Print.

4 – Obedience > Outcome

1. Hubbard, Ginger. *I Can't Believe You Just Said That!: Biblical Wisdom for Taming Your Child's Tongue.* Nashville: Nelson Books, 2018. Print.

5 – With God > For God

1. Story shared with permission; name changed to protect confidentiality.

6 – Godfidence > Confidence

1. "Definition of confidence." *Oxford University Press.* Lexico.com.

7 – Purpose > Preference

1. Myers, *Famous In Heaven & At Home.*

8 – Faith > Fear

1. Spurgeon, Charles. "Faith is Made Up of Three Things." *Reasons for Hope* Jesus*, 13 March 2021. <https:// reasonsforhopejesus.com/faith-is-made-up-of-three-things-knowledge-belief-and-trust>

9 – Growth Focused > Goal Focused

1. Tozer, A.W. *The Pursuit of God.* Harrisburg: Christian Publications, 1948. Print.
2. Bridges, Jerry. *The Discipline of Grace: God's Role and Our Role in the Pursuit of Holiness.* Colorado Springs: NavPress, 1994. Print.
3. TerKeurst, Lysa. *Made to Crave.* Zondervan, 2010. Print.

10 – Humility > Pride

1. Hedges, Brian. *Hit List: Taking Aim at the Seven Deadly Sins.* Minneapolis: Cruciform, 2014. Print.
2. Lucado, Max. "Pride – The Poison Pill." *Max Lucado*, May 2016. <https://maxlucado.com/pride-poison-pill>

11 – Honor Your Body > Accept Your Body
1. "Definitions of Accepting and Honoring." *Oxford University Press*. Lexico.com.
2. Piper, John. "The Renewed Mind and How to Have It." *desiringGod*, 15 August 2004. <https://www.desiringgod.org/messages/the-renewed-mind-and-how-to-have-it>

12 – Discipline > Motivation
1. "What Does The Bible Say About Motivation?" *GotQuestions*. <https://www.gotquestions.org/Bible-motivation.html>
2. Eldredge, John. *Walking With God*. Nashville: Thomas Nelson, 2008. Print.
3. Piper, John. "True Freedom Begins with Your Mind." *desiringGod*, 15 June 2017. <https://www.desiringgod.org/messages/the-renewed-mind-and-how-to-have-it/excerpts/true-freedom-begins-with-your-mind>
4. Quote credited to Abraham Lincoln.
5. Somer Phoebus quote from "She Works His Way" seminar workshop.
6. Manuel, Sam. "3 Ways to Embrace Spiritual Training and Discipline." *Deep Spirituality*, 2 August 2021. <https://deepspirituality.com/spiritual-training>

13 – Holiness > Freedom
1. Whittle, Lisa. *Jesus Over Everything.* Nashville: W Publishing Group, 2020. Print.
2. Tripp, Paul. "The Doctrine of Holiness." *Paul Tripp*, 10 September 2018. <https://www.paultripp.com/articles/posts/the-doctrine-of-holiness-article>

3. Piper, John. "The Renewed Mind and How to Have It." *desiringGod*, 15 August 2004. <https://www.desiringgod.org/messages/the-renewed-mind-and-how-to-have-it>

4. Stedman, Ray. "Legalism." *Ray Stedman, Authentic Christianity*, 14 May 1972. <https://www.raystedman.org/thematic-studies/new-covenant/legalism>

14 – Beliefs > Behavior

1. TerKeurst, Lysa. *Made to Crave*. Zondervan, 2010. Print.

16 – His Way = The Way

1. Quote from Christine Cain during the 2021 IF:Gathering live event.

Made in the USA
Middletown, DE
07 June 2023

32225748R00135